Elżbieta Adamska

TOP
100
RECIPES
OF TRADITIONAL
POLISH CUISINE

fk WYDAWNICTWO OLESIEJUK

Contents

Introduction

In Poland there is a well-known saying, "Proverbs are the wisdom of nations". Like most Poles I have heard the proverb, "The grass is greener on the other side of the fence" meaning that we undervalue familiar things and may not even know what treasures we possess. One such treasure is Polish cuisine. It is rarely featured in restaurants, which usually offer "universal" dishes, although such local delicacies as *kartacze* (potato dumplings with minced meat, also known as *cepelinai*), *kolduny* (dough dumplings stuffed with meat) and *kolaczki* (sweet cakes with cheese filling) are served more and more often. By the way, I have eaten excellent Kashubian herrings in the mountain town Zakopane, and Silesian dumplings by the seaside in Łeba, which leads me to the conclusion that few regions are able to turn their traditional delicacies into tourist attractions – Cracow bagels, pastry roosters from Kazimierz, and *oscypek*, sheep's milk cheese from Zakopane, are notable exceptions to this rule.

However, lately I've been seeing some positive signs: we are increasingly aware of the importance of healthy eating. A good example is eating seasonal produce, which guarantees the highest quality. In spring, asparagus will be firm, crunchy and fresh, but tomatoes smell and taste best in summer, plucked straight from the bush. The plentiful autumn harvest offers us succulent beets, pumpkins, apples and plums, whereas in winter, dried mushrooms perfectly complement a pot of sour rye soup, borscht or thick sauce.

We know that produce grown in our area will be fresher, but buying regional products isn't always feasible in the city. Globalization means that it's easier to buy strawberries from Portugal than local ones; however, I have created my own large base of reliable regional suppliers of wholesome food products. I truly enjoy the days when I have time to visit the marketplace. I love talking to the sellers – of apples, for example. No one knows as much about the fruit as they do. They will advise the buyer which apple varieties to choose and how to store them.

A walk through the marketplace is pure pleasure. Here, time has stopped: you can buy herrings straight from the barrel, delicious sauerkraut, and equally tasty fermented cucumbers. You are surrounded by a profusion of choices and all the products are of the highest quality: from carrots, parsley and pumpkins to smoked eels, whitefish and vendace.

"Do not be shocked that in this first book of mine I start out with Polish dishes (...) for I truly think you ought to taste the old Polish dishes first, and should you find they do not satisfy your appetite, I will send you on to other, more special ones".

So wrote Stanisław Czerniecki in 1682 in his *Compendium ferculorum*, one of the first cookbooks describing the dishes of Polish cuisine.

What are the specialities of our cookery? Dishes made from cabbage – or so one might assume after looking at statistical data regarding shopping preferences. However, foreigners usually say that soups constitute the strongest point of Polish cuisine. Cabbage soup is one example, but red borscht, split pea soup, mushroom soup, barley soup and sour rye soup are also very popular.

How can one distinguish genuine Polish dishes from those which are a product of foreign influences? Are the dishes prepared during the period when Poland was partitioned, under foreign rule, really ours? After all, cultural influences have been manifold throughout our history, marked by wars and loss of independence, changing fashions and poverty. Thus, first of all I eliminated all the products typical for the cuisines of other countries. It is true that Poland is not famous for its cheeses – even though the name of Tilsiter cheese comes from the town Tilsit in East Prussia, according to sources it was Swiss settlers who popularized this type of cheese and adapted the production method to local conditions. On the other hand, we do make wonderful Korycin cheeses and *oscypek*. Furthermore, for hundreds of years we have prepared fresh cottage cheese for our children by heating fermented milk. Thus, it is necessary to determine which dishes and food products are inherently ours, developed on our territory, and have been a part of our cuisine for generations, like *zrazy* (meat roulade with buckwheat groats), tripe soup or *pierogi*, and which ones are obviously imported, like carrots, celery and parsley. Are pancakes more typical for French or Polish culinary culture? Are they the favourite dish of many Poles precisely because we have been preparing them for centuries? When did we begin to cultivate sweet peppers and why do we associate this plant with Hungarian cuisine? And the Bretons have never heard of "Breton baked beans", which are so popular in Poland.

Today, when products from all over the world are easily available, the greatest strength of Polish cuisine still lies in old customs such as the meatless Christmas Eve Supper (a delight for the palate and a tribute to tradition), or food blessing at Easter. However, the fast pace of modern life means that we rarely prepare stuffed pike, eels in dill sauce, or many other time-consuming delicacies which were once the pride of Polish cookery. Luckily, certain traditional food products – such as groats, rye flour, linseed oil and lacto-fermented vegetables – are regaining popularity; a good thing, since they are healthy, widely available and tasty.

Here, I will describe simple dishes such as *krupnik* (barley soup), *bigos* (cabbage stew) and *pierogi*, which are always met with enthusiasm, regardless of the age or personal preferences of the eater. It is foods such as Polish herring, *zrazy*, red beets and *mazurek* cake that make Polish cookery so worthy of interest.

Herring in oil

4 herring fillets

1 onion

   a few allspice seeds

2 bay leaves

¾ glass of olive oil or
   preferred oil

   pepper

Herring in oil is readily available in shops. If you buy it there, all you need to do is cut the fish into pieces, add layers of finely chopped onion (preferably scalded in a sieve to get rid of piquancy and soften it up a bit), allspice, pepper, a bay leaf, then steep in oil and put aside for 24 hours in the fridge.

A better option, though, would be to find real, meaty herring (matjes) sold whole, as it is much more tasty. The fish should be soaked for 24 hours, with the water changed several times, and then cut along the stomach and gutted. If you find milt or spawn, do not throw away this delicacy. It can be used as the basis for an excellent sauce, significantly improving this fish. The next step is to skin it, making a nick at the tail and carefully pulling the skin off all the way to the head, which we cut off and throw away. Then cut the fish into two fillets, starting at the tail and slowly boning it. After that, follow the instructions given above.

This basic recipe can be modified by adding finely chopped garlic, thin lemon slices, or thin lemon strands made using a citrus zester. The fish tastes great sprinkled with layers of marjoram and baked white beans (they can be canned, but these need to be rinsed in a sieve to get rid of the thick, rich sauce). If we use herring in spiced brine, the taste will be a little different. You can serve it on a platter, garnished with finely chopped onion. To turn it into a legitimate appetizer, all you need to do is place pieces of herring on slices of cooled jacked potato, sprinkle with finely chopped onion, and top with a dollop of sauce (mustard, mayonnaise) and half a slice of lemon or a sprig of dill.

To make herring in a milt sauce, simply blend milt or spawn with a pinch of icing sugar and a tbsp of lemon sauce or mustard. You can add 2 tbsp of sour cream. Spawn needs a lemon sauce and olive or regular oil.

Rollmops

8 herring fillets in oil

8 toothpicks

1 onion

2 sizeable gherkins

2 tbsp of mustard

Marinade:

1 glass of water

½ glass of white vinegar

2 bay leaves

a few seeds of allspice

a few peppercorns

a pinch of salt

Bring to the boil.

Place fillets skin down on a chopping board and spread mustard on the inside. Put a piece of a gherkin cut lengthwise in four, roll up tightly and secure with a toothpick. Place the rollmops in a dish, cover with sliced or chopped onion and steep in the cooled marinade. They are ready to serve the next day.

There are different versions of this basic recipe. You can stuff the fish with dried tomatoes, onion, a sprig of dill, or a piece of cheese or asparagus. Rollmops are also delicious in a marinade made with cream, mayonnaise, olive oil and lemon juice (shake the ingredients well in a closed jar), garnish with a sprig of dill before serving. You can cover them with a cream blanket, adding an apple. Grate a washed and peeled sour apple on a large-hole grater, mix with lemon juice to preserve its colour, and with clotted cream. Those who prefer more spicy dishes can add a clove of garlic, strained through a garlic press. The sauce can be modified, combining cream with mayonnaise or mixing it with onion sweated in butter.

A marinade can be made with mustard shaken with oil and a pinch of herbs, or with a tomato sauce seasoned with hot spices. Cook someeat leek slowly in clarified butter with one finely chopped celery stalk, remove from the heat and mix with tomato paste, spicy ketchup, salt, a pinch of dried pepper, a drop of lemon juice and a pinch of sugar. and you will have another version of the garnish. In the Kaszuby region finely chopped pickled cucumbers are added to the marinade of stewed onion. I've also eaten herring with cooked, dried mushrooms.

Herring with beets

½ kg of beets
4 herring fillets in oil
1 large onion
1 glass of olive oil
a few seeds of allspice
1 bay leaf
pepper
1 tsp of marjoram
juice from ½ a lemon

Boil the washed and unpeeled beetroot in water with a vegetable stock cube, or bake it in the oven (to make it sweeter). Cool it and cut into thin slices if they are small, or half-slices if they are larger. Sprinkle beets with juice squeezed from half a lemon to keep its vivid colour. Chop the onion finely.

Place layers of beet, onion, spices and herring (cut into pieces) in a dish. Pour enough olive oil to fill all gaps and cover the dish. Set aside in the fridge for a couple of hours to let the flavours blend well.

If you cut the herring into cubes and place in the middle of a dish, you will have the basis for a fish tartare. It's a good idea to surround it with a finely chopped shallot, beets cut in smaller pieces, green peas, pieces of hard-boiled egg, olives, chopped gherkins and other ingredients to your liking.

Stuffed fish

1 kg of various fish fillets

1 small white bread roll

1 glass of milk

  soup vegetables

1 vegetable stock cube

2 onions

1 tbsp of butter

  a few seeds of allspice

1 bay leaf

  salt, pepper

  marjoram

1 tbsp of finely chopped dill
or parsley

1 egg

  gelatine

Soak the roll in milk (or thick stock). Boil the vegetable stock, adding allspice, a bay leaf and vegetable stock cubes, in a small amount of water. Once the vegetables are tender, remove them. Cook the onion slowly in butter in a frying pan and season with salt.

Mince the fish (rinsed and well drained), onion and the firmly pressed roll. Add spices, dill or parsley, marjoram and a whole egg. Season with salt and pepper, mix. If the dish is too soft, you can add a ablespoontbspbsp of breadcrumbs. Shape it into a roll with a diameter of about 10 cm. Spread some oil on a linen cloth and place the fish stuffing on it. Shape it into a roll and secure both ends. Another way is to put it into a nylon sleeve, prepared beforehand, and knot or sew up the ends, or wrap the stuffing in a layer of gauze. Put it into clear broth and cook for a quarter of an hour or so. Leave it in to cool, then cut the "sleeve" and divide the roll into centimetre-wide slices with a sharp knife. Arrange on a dish, garnish with carrot or the same way as with the jellied fish. Mix soaked gelatine (prepared according to the instructions on the packaging) with the strained broth, leave to cool and pour over fish.

To simplify the process you can shape the fish stuffing into balls the size of a large walnut using wet hands and cook them in the broth. The dish will be even better if you place soaked raisins and pieces of walnut on the serving plate before you steep the fish in the broth. You can also cut slightly defrosted fillets instead of mincing them, and proceed according to the instructions.

You can add variety to the stuffing by including a few finely chopped mushrooms to the fried onion.

In Lvov they used to serve balls made according to this recipe, only covered with the sauce of soaked, dried plums, cooked until tender, strained through a sieve and seasoned with lemon juice or wine, with a pinch of sugar, salt and pepper, and a tablespoontbsp tbspof mayonnaise.

Jellied fish

1 kg of carp or other fish

1 litre of thick vegetable
  broth (you can use
  a vegetable stock cube)

1 bay leaf

  a few seeds of allspice

1 onion

1 carrot

¼ of celeriac

1 sprig of parsley

  sugar, salt, pepper

  parsley leaves to garnish

Make thick vegetable broth from soup vegetables or cook vegetables until tender in a small amount of water, adding onion, a bay leaf, allspice and a vegetable stock cube. Take the vegetables out, season with salt and pepper and cook the scaled fish, cut into pieces, for 20 minutes. Don't forget to include fins and head, otherwise the broth won't set. After you cool it down and check to see if there are any bones left that can be removed, place the fish on a dish, garnish it with slices of carrot and sprigs of parsley. Strain the broth through a thick sieve, add a pinch of sugar (the broth should be cool and congealing) and pour it over the fish. After a couple of hours in the fridge it will set into jelly. You can decorate the dish with green peas, slices of lemon and hard-boiled egg. When using fish less glutinous than carp, add gelatine (preferably leaves) soaked in cold water (see instructions on the packaging).

If you don't need the jelly to be clear, you can add blended onion cooked in the broth, which will subtly spice up the fish.

4 pig's trotters

   soup vegetables

2 bay leaves

   a few seeds of allspice

1 onion

   a few sprigs of parsley

1 tsp of marjoram

2 garlic cloves

1 tbsp of lemon juice

   salt, pepper

   a pinch of sugar

Pig's trotters in aspic

Put the well-cleaned trotters into a pot, cover with water, add bay leaves and allspice and cook over a low heat for at least an hour (depending on the portion size and quality of the meat). Add the vegetables, onion, garlic and salt and cook for another 40 minutes. Remove the carrot earlier, so that it is firm and not overcooked, since it will be used as a garnish. The meat should be tender. Season with marjoram, salt and pepper. Strain the broth and leave to cool a little. Separate meat from bones (throw the bones away) and cut into small pieces. Put the meat into little moulds, add sliced carrot and parsley leaves. Cover with setting jelly. You don't need much, and there won't be a lot left after such long cooking anyway. Set aside in the fridge and, before you serve, garnish the small pyramids, removed from moulds, with segments of lemon.

This traditional and very tasty dish is a rare presence on our tables as it is time-consuming to make. Calf's-foot takes much less time to cook. You can also make jelly from turkey using this recipe, but in order for it to be glutinous and congeal you have to dissolve it in a small amount of liquid or mix it with gelatine, dissolved as per the instructions on the packaging.

Tenderloin carpaccio

Rub the rinsed and dried meat with a mixture of olive oil, bay leaf, ground seeds of allspice, Provençal herbs and a clove of garlic strained through a garlic press. Set it aside in the fridge for at least 24 hours, but to make the tenderloin seasoned this way really delicious, leave it there for a few days. Turn it frequently so that it gets evenly covered with the grey coating.

You can also marinade it in a mixture of oil and soup vegetables, grated using a large-hole grater, and spices, i.e. a few juniper berries, allspice and marjoram. Don't forget to turn the meat so that it is evenly covered with the marinade. Before serving put it in the freezer compartment for a short while, as it will then be easier to cut thin slices. Put these slices flat on a serving dish, top with Parmesan cheese freshly grated using a grater with medium holes. You should serve good quality oil, balsamic vinegar and freshly ground pepper separately. Don't pour sauces over the meat as this takes away the aroma and character of the marinade.

You can garnish the dish with pickled mushrooms or capers.

½ kg of beef tenderloin
a few seeds of allspice
1 bay leaf
1 clove of garlic
1 tsp of Provençal herbs
3 tbsp of olive oil
2 tbsp of white wine vinegar
salt, pepper
2 tbsp of freshly grated Parmesan cheese

Steak tartare

Choosing the right meat is the key. It has to be tender and not marbled. Don't mince tenderloin into a pulp, but thoroughly chop it with a sharp knife. You should serve oil and grated Parmesan cheese separately (it's best to buy a chunk of cheese and grate it using a grater with medium holes, to make sure it is fresh and aromatic).

Traditionally Steak tartare is accompanied by finely cut gherkins (or pickled mushrooms) and onion. However, chanterelle mushrooms fried in cream will turn this dish into a real treat.

Cookeat finely chopped onion in butter, add thoroughly washed and chopped mushrooms, season with salt and pepper and cook for 20 minutes without the lid on (so that the sauce is not too watery). Finally, blend with fat cream. You can also fry the mushrooms in butter without onion and cream.

To obtain a more sophisticated flavour, buy meat one day in advance and rub it thoroughly with herbs (ground juniper berriesseeds, allspice, one clove and one bay leaf) mixed with a tbsp of oil.

You should put the yolks into shallow holes pressed into the raw meat (they can also be served separately, so that everyone can choose their preferred proportions of ingredients and season the meat to their liking with oil, lemon juice, freshly ground pepper and Parmesan cheese). Steak tartare can also be garnished with caviar.

½ kg of beef tenderloin

olive oil

1 lemon

2 yolks

2 tbsp of Parmesan cheese

4 gherkins

250 g of chanterelle or other mushrooms

2 tbsp of fat cream

1 tbsp of butter

2 onions or chives

salt, pepper

Stuffed eggs

6 eggs

1 large onion or a bunch of spring onions

50 g of butter

2 tbsp of breadcrumbs

salt, pepper

Hard-boil eggs (put them into cold, salted water and boil over a low heat so that the eggshells don't break). Cool and cut in half with one decisive motion. Take out the insides delicately, preserving the eggshells. Melt half the butter in a frying pan and fry the finely chopped onion. It will be ready faster if you add salt to it. Remove from the heat, add the finely chopped eggs, season with salt and pepper and fry with the onion for a little while. Put the stuffing into the empty shells and sprinkle with breadcrumbs. Melt the rest of the butter in the frying pan and place the eggs shell up. Fry for a few minutes over a low heat until they turn light brown. Serve warm or cold.

You can modify this basic recipe by adding finely chopped mushrooms and finely chopped parsley leaves or dill to the stuffing.

Eggs stuffed with pastes

6 eggs

pastes (various types)

Cut hard-boiled and peeled eggs in half, carefully remove yolks and make the paste, which will be put back in the yolks' place.

There is a wide selection of pastes you can use:

- a cheese paste is made by mixing yolks with a cheese spread (100 g), one tbsp of mayonnaise, one tbsp of oil and spices to taste;
- an anchovy paste is made by mixing yolks with a tbsp of oil, a tbsp of mayonnaise, a few anchovies, a tbsp of lemon juice and a pinch of freshly ground pepper;
- a fish paste is made with smoked fish instead of anchovies;
- a peanut paste is made by browning a handful of peanuts in a dry frying pan and then mixing them with 3 tbsp of olive oil, 1 tbsp of pitted olives, a yolk, pepper, a tbsp of lemon juice and a few leaves of sweet basil.

Garnishing these eggs is a great opportunity to show off your skills. They look appetizing arranged on lettuce leaves. Red roe will bring out their uniqueness, and a sprig of dill will highlight the subtle, silky flavour of the pastes.

Tenderloin in butter

Put the meat (rinsed and dried with membranes removed) into a saucepan with melted butter and garlic strained through a garlic press. Fry for 20 minutes over a low heat turning evenly to prevent the butter from burning.

Once cool the fat can be used for sauces. Rub the meat with freshly ground pepper and salt, wrap in aluminium foil and leave in the fridge so that it is easier to cut it into slices before serving. Tenderloin prepared according to this recipe should be well-done on the outside, but pale pink inside. It shouldn't be raw, however, like meat intended for carpaccio. It can be served with sauces, but thanks to its subtle, buttery flavour, it tastes great on its own.

1 kg of tenderloin

2 cloves of garlic

200 g of butter

½ a tsp of freshly ground pepper, salt

Plums in bacon

Wrap the soft, dried plums tightly in thin, narrow bacon strips and hold in place with a toothpick. Arrange on a roasting tin and place in a hot oven for a couple of minutes. The bacon should be browned slightly. Serve hot. This is one of the easiest and most delicious snacks.

If the plums are dry, you need to soak them beforehand, preferably in sherry.

For a similar effect, bake figs cut in half and wrap in strips of semi-dried ham.

200 g of pitted dried plums

a few thin slices of lean bacon

toothpicks

Asparagus with a sauce

Asparagus, a delicacy in many countries, is cooked in butter, fried, served in soups, or with Hollandaise sauce. However, to prepare asparagus Polish-style, follow the recipe below:

1 bunch of asparagus

2 tbsp of butter

1 tbsp of breadcrumbs

1 tsp of sugar, salt

Just wash the green stalks, cutting off the hard ends. White asparagus requires removing the hard skin (from the tip down). This vegetable should be cooked in a special-purpose, tall pot with a sieve, as the tips are ready after a couple of minutes, whereas the bottom part of the stalk takes much longer. Cook the stalks in salted water with a pinch of sugar, not too long though, so that they remain firm and slightly crunchy. Put the breadcrumbs in a small frying pan, heated without any fat, and when they are slightly brown, add the butter. In this way the breadcrumbs will absorb less fat. Put the cooked asparagus on a serving dish and pour the butter with breadcrumbs over it.

It also tastes great with finely chopped, hard-boiled eggs.

You can also use the same recipe for cauliflower, broccoli, Brussels sprouts, green string beans or other vegetables cooked in water.

Chicken liver pâté

Melt the butter in a frying pan, fry onions cut in halved slices, add herbs, and after a few minutes also the rinsed and dried livers. Don't salt the onion as blue cheese is quite salty anyway. Fry the meat until well done, stirring constantly so that it doesn't stay raw inside. Cool it and mince, adding the cheese. Mix with brandy and thick cream. Finally, season with freshly ground pepper, herbs and salt if needed. Spread oil over the surface of a bowl, put the meat in and set aside in the fridge for the pâté to congeal. Before serving all you need to do is keep the dish in warm hands for a while and the pâté will separate from the dish turned upside down. You can garnish it with a ring of green olives or dried tomatoes in brine.

½ kg of chicken livers

2 large onions

2 tbsp of butter

50 ml of brandy

200 ml of cream

100 g of Rokpol (Polish blue ch or other blue cheese

½ a tsp of coarsely ground bl pepper

1 tsp of herbs (marjoram, oregano, thyme)

1 tbsp of oil

Duck pâté

1 whole duck

200 g of poultry livers

1 onion

2 tbsp of clarified butter

200 ml of thick cream

2 eggs

a few slices of smoked bacon

1 glass of brandy or plum
vodka – 25 ml

1 tbsp of marjoram

1 clove of garlic

salt, pepper

Rub the rinsed and dried duck with marjoram, salt and pepper, and roast until tender (I roast it for 90 minutes on a rack to melt a large proportion of the fat). Remove the skin, separate the meat from the bones and mince with onion fried in clarified butter and livers. Mix with cream, add a glass of alcohol, garlic strained through a garlic press, salt and pepper, and finally yolks with egg whites whipped to a froth. Place this mixture in a mould and cover with thin slices of bacon. Place in a hot oven at 180°C for 45 minutes, preferably covered with foil, and then remove the foil and roast until the bacon is brown.

Although pâté originated in France this dish has enjoyed unwavering popularity in Poland, too, in particular as regards duck and game pâté. Roasted and steamed, baked in short-crust pastry, French pastry, raised cake, flavoured with porcini mushrooms, brandy or juniper. Served cold and fried with chopped onion. Usually it is served with cranberry preserves or cowberry jam, but my favourite is pâté with a sauce made with: 1 tbsp of plum jam, 1 tbsp of rosehip jam, 1 tbsp of candied orange peel, 1 tbsp of pickled plums, cut into small pieces, and 1 tbsp of the sauce from those plums.

Mix and serve with cold, cured meat.

In the past, a speciality of many households was goose neck filled with stuffing made of offal with parsley leaves and fried onion. It was roasted together with a goose in a roasting tin, with both its ends sewn up.

A fresh take on duck pâté

Pickle the duck breast (rinsed, drained with skin removed) and livers in a marinade of oil, bay leaf, allspice, pepper, brandy, juice squeezed from an orange and honey for 24 hours. Mince in a blender with the ingredients of the marinade, mix with the yolk, cream, orange peel, an ingredient of choice (pistachio nuts, porcini mushrooms, plums or raisins) and clarified butter. Season with salt, and at the end add egg whites whipped to a stiff froth. Spread a mould with butter, put the dish in and roast it in the oven (covering the top with a piece of foil). Similarly to the recipe above, you can cover the mould with strips of bacon or pork fat. Another option is to grease it with butter and sprinkle with breadcrumbs to get a crunchy crust.

4 duck breasts

a few seeds of allspice

1 glass of brandy – 25 ml

2 tbsp of olive oil

1 tbsp of honey

1 tsp of pepper

200 g of poultry liver

1 tbsp of clarified butter

1 egg

200 ml of thick cream

choose from: a handful of shelled pistachio nuts, stewed porcini mushrooms, dried plums or raisins

orange juice

peel from one orange

200 ml of thick cream

1 bay leaf

salt, pepper

1 kg of various types of meat
(beef, pork, turkey)

300 g of liver (calf's liver is the best,
but poultry liver will do, too)

1 clove of garlic

1 vegetable stock cube

2 carrots

1 sprig of parsley

1 small celeriac

1 onion

2 tbsp of butter

2 tbsp of oil

50 ml of brandy or plum vodka

1 egg

½ tsp of marjoram

½ tsp of oregano

1 tbsp of mustard

a few strips of smoked bacon

salt, pepper

Meat pâté

I used to cook the meat in separate pots, seasoning each with a slightly different mixture of herbs. Since I make much smaller portions these days I stew pieces of beef and pork together (I put them into hot fat with a clove of garlic cut in slices and brown them all over, adding a glass of hot water with a cube of vegetable broth dissolved in it). After one hour I add poultry and vegetables cut into small pieces, stewing for another hour. I cook half-slices of onion and liver in butter, adding spices. When the meat cools, mince it with vegetables and their own sauce, as well as with liver and onion – thanks to the vegetables the pâté will not be too dry. Now add a tbsp of mustard, yolk, a glass of alcohol, season to taste and finally add egg whites whipped to a froth. Cover a mould with strips of bacon, put the dish in, wrap with bacon and put an additional strip on top. Place in a heated oven for an hour until the bacon is brown.

A fresh take on meat pâté

Rinse the meat, cut into small pieces, place in a small amount of boiling water, cook until tender, adding a vegetable stock cube, bay leaves and allspice. Fry rinsed liver in oil or olive oil. Drain the meat off and mince in a meat mincer, adding raw bacon and fried liver. Mix with raw eggs (beat egg whites to a froth) and cream, season with nutmeg, salt, pepper or other spices of choice. Cover the roasting tin with strips of smoked bacon, leaving the tips outside, place minced meat on top of it and cover with the tips of bacon strips. Cover with aluminium foil, roast for 45 minutes at 180°C.

300 g of boned veal

200 g of pork blade

100 g of raw bacon

400 g of smoked bacon cut into
strips

150 g of calf's or poultry liver

2 tbsp of oil

2 eggs

2 tbsp of cream

2 bay leaves

a few seeds of allspice

a pinch of nutmeg

a vegetable stock cube, salt,
pepper

Terrine of hare

1 skinned hare

100 g of lard

   soup vegetables

1 onion

2 bay leaves

600 g of raw or smoked bacon

200 g of pork liver

½ litre of vegetable stock

1 stale white bread roll

2 eggs

½ tsp of marjoram

½ tsp of thyme

½ tsp of ground ginger

2 cloves

   a few seeds of allspice, salt, pepper

Fry the finely chopped soup vegetables in a saucepan in lard, add the meat of a rinsed, dried and filleted hare, bay leaves and allspice and stew for about an hour until tender, adding a little of vegetable broth.

The terrine will be much more tasty if you add offal, namely heart, liver and lungs. Otherwise, fry pork liver, add to the hare and stew together. Add the bacon, cooked earlier. When the meat is tender, put aside to cool and then mince everything together, adding the roll, soaked in the broth and pressed. Season with salt, pepper, thyme, marjoram, ginger and two ground cloves. Mix with two raw eggs and place the kneaded meat in a mould covered with bacon strips or baking paper. Put in a heated oven and roast for 60 minutes at a moderate temperature.

Potato salad

½ kg of potatoes

2 gherkins

1 onion or spring onion with chives

2 tbsp of mayonnaise

1 tbsp of spicy mustard

1 tbsp of finely chopped parsley leaves

salt, pepper

This salad was introduced in our country by Queen Bona, but didn't catch on for many years. Nowadays, it is served in all shapes and sizes in almost every restaurant. Salads made from cooked vegetables with mayonnaise are unwaveringly popular, as you can prepare them beforehand and store for several days.

Boil the potatoes in their skins, washing them first and cooking in a small amount of water, add salt at the end, drain off and leave to cool. Peel and cut into cubes.

Add finely chopped gherkins and one big or two smaller chopped spring onions with chives and a tbsp of parsley leaves.

Mix with two tbsp of mayonnaise and one tbsp of spicy mustard, and season with salt and pepper. You can add variety to the salad with capers, green peas (boiled or canned), ham cut into small pieces, roasted meat or herrings in oil, as well as hard-boiled eggs, dill and peeled apples cut into small pieces.

Pickled beet salad

Peel the boiled and cooled beets and cut them into slices, or half-slices if large, and then place them in a jar. Bring the wine with wine vinegar, cloves, bay leaf, allspice and finely chopped onion to the boil. Season with salt, sugar and pepper. Steep the beets in the marinade, add dried plums, cut in half, screw the lid on, shake well and set aside for 24 hours in the fridge. Before serving take out the beets, onion and plums, throw away the spices and mix some of the sauce with the horseradish and olive oil, season and pour over the salad.

Grated cold beetroot with horseradish is a traditional addition to meat dishes. It is made from cooked or baked beetroot grated using a sieve (thick or with larger holes) with salt, sugar, horseradish, cumin and lemon juice.

½ kg of baked beets

¾ glass of dry red wine

100 ml of red wine vinegar

1 red onion

a handful of dried plums

3 cloves

a few seeds of allspice

1 bay leaf

2 tbsp of oil

½ tsp of horseradish

salt, pepper

a pinch of sugar

Stuffed savoy cabbage leaves

8 savoy cabbage leaves

1 l of vegetable stock (or
   a stock cube dissolved in
   boiling water)

8 slices of smoked ham

8 tsp of herb spread

2 tbsp of lemon juice

2 tbsp of dill

   salt, pepper, sugar

Remove outer leaves from a head of the cabbage, throwing away flawed ones. If the cabbage is compact, you have to scald it in a bowl, cut off the leaves at the stalk and delicately separate them from it. It's a good idea to use the rest of the leaves to make stuffed cabbage.

Bring the broth to the boil and cook leaves until tender, remove and cool. Cut off thickened nerves, flatten the leaves out on a cutting board, spread with cheese (seasoned with salt, pepper and, optionally, a pinch of sugar), cover with a slice of ham and roll up. You can shape them like a croquette or stuffed cabbage, i.e. fold leaf sides inside and tightly roll up, or make a roll and cut into smaller rolls. Sprinkle with lemon juice and garnish with chopped dill.

Such rolls used to be served with a home-made cream instead of the spread. It was made from whipped cream with icing sugar, mixed with horseradish and a yolk strained through a sieve.

If you cut the leaves in half, you will get great tiny croquettes.

It only takes a few minutes to prepare all kinds of small rolls: wrap pieces of soft goat's cheese and a slice of dried fig in a smoked, slightly dried ham, a slice of smoked salmon covered with the herb spread, and a cucumber cut into thin slices, and then slide it into a rolled lettuce leaf filled with mini-salad.

Omelette with onion and vegetables

The omelette owes its ultimate perfection and fame to French masters of the culinary art, but it was known as early as in ancient Rome, and has also been popular in our parts for centuries, served with salty and sweet flavours. It tastes best straight from the frying pan.

2 eggs

1 tbsp of flour

1 tbsp of milk

2 tbsp of butter

1 onion

1 tomato

¼ of a bell pepper or several slices of courgette

salt, pepper

a pinch of dried basil

Mix whole eggs with milk, salt and flour. If done thoroughly, it will produce a smooth dough, which after baking should look like a pancake. If, however, the ingredients are not blended well, in places it will resemble scrambled eggs. Heat butter or other fat in a second frying pan and fry the onion, adding salt to speed up the process, with peeled tomato and courgette, seasoning with pepper and a pinch of ground basil or a few finely chopped fresh basil leaves at the end.

When the dough in the first frying pan sets, put the stuffing on half of it and cover with the other half, fold at the centre, fry for a while longer and slide onto a plate.

If an omelette sticks to a frying pan, lift its ridges with a wide knife and shake the frying pan, but this shouldn't happen if you remember to pour the dough onto well-heated fat and spread it evenly.

You can modify this omelette recipe, adding grated cheese to the dough and slices of ham or favourite ingredients to the stuffing.

To make a really special omelette, first fry vegetables in a frying pan (one by one, as they get tender) and pour whisked eggs over them.

$\mathcal{S}$ponge omelette

2 eggs

1 tbsp of flour

1 tbsp of milk

1 tbsp of butter

 a pinch of salt

1 pack of vanilla sugar

Using the ingredients listed above you can make a completely different omelette if you just separate yolks from whites and whisk them to a froth. First thoroughly mix yolks, milk, salt and vanilla sugar (optional) with flour, and add egg whites whipped to a froth at the end. Mix carefully and pour into a hot frying pan with melted fat – not too hot, though, since butter burns easily. After a few minutes flip the omelette over. You can toss it into the air, but I don't recommend it to beginners. You should use a wide spatula, sliding it carefully under the well risen, fluffy dough.

This sweet omelette (with a slightly brown edge and a buttery aroma) tastes best with preserves, icing sugar or thick fruit syrup.

If you appreciate a buttery flavour, you can add a tbsp of melted butter and a tbsp of cream to the dough.

Drop scones with apples

Their origins date back to regional cuisine. They used to be made from groats, potatoes and flour, and served with a salty or sweet flavour.

2 eggs

1 glass of sour milk

1 glass of flour

½ tsp of baking powder

2 apples

  frying fat

2 tbsp of icing sugar

1 pack of vanilla sugar

  salt

Add sour milk, flour, a pinch of salt and baking powder to whisked raw eggs. Mix into a dough with the consistency of thick cream and set aside for half an hour. Grate peeled apples using a big-hole grater, mix with the dough, which is then put on heated fat, forming scones. Fry on both sides until golden. Remove from the frying pan onto a plate (you can leave them on a paper towel for a while to drain off the excess fat), sprinkle with icing sugar mixed with vanilla sugar.

They will be more fluffy if you whisk the egg whites into a froth.

In the salty version don't add baking powder. Instead mix the dough with grated courgette. You can garnish them with a sprig of dill and sprinkle with coarsely ground pepper, serve with tomato sauce or chanterelle mushrooms stewed in cream.

Bean soup

a few slices of smoked bacon

250 g of beans

1 onion

1 clove of garlic

soup vegetables

1 bay leaf

a few seeds of allspice

2 tbsp of olive oil

2 tbsp of lemon juice

1 chilli pepper

1 tsp of oregano

1 tsp of marjoram

½ tsp of ground cumin

2 large potatoes

salt, pepper and sugar
to taste

Soak the washed beans overnight (the type depends on individual taste; you don't need to soak young beans). Cook in the same water, adding soup vegetables, a bay leaf and allspice. Cooking time depends on the type of beans. They should be cooked over a low heat so that the beans don't break. If you want to serve the soup with potatoes, wash them, peel, cut into cubes and add at the end of cooking the beans. The potatoes will be tender within 10 minutes from the moment you put them into boiling water.

Cut the smoked bacon into pieces, add finely chopped onion and garlic, and fry in olive oil for about 10 minutes, until slightly brown. Season with finely chopped chilli pepper, cumin, oregano and marjoram. Mix together and add to the cooked beans and potatoes. Season the dish to taste with salt, pepper, lemon juice and sugar.

Fans of bean soup with *łazanki* (Polish type of short pasta) should cook the pasta separately, according to package instructions.

If you are going to eat the whole dish at once, you can add a little water from cooking the pasta to the soup. If you don't plan on adding smoked bacon, you can improve the taste of the soup with a roux from butter (1 tbsp) melted in a saucepan and flour (1 tbsp) browned in it. Then mix the roux gradually with a small amount of soup and add to the rest.

You can use the same recipe to make pea soup. A soup seasoned with spices, made from green string beans cut into smaller pieces with soup vegetables and smoked bacon, cut into smaller pieces, as in the recipe above, is not only delicious, but also easily digestible.

Tomato soup

1 kg of tomatoes

soup vegetables

1 bay leaf

a few seeds of allspice

1 clove of garlic (or more)

1 tsp of Provençal herbs

1 tbsp of buckwheat honey

1 tbsp of lemon juice
(or orange juice)

a pinch of powdered pepper

a few leaves of fresh basil

salt, pepper

Prepare a strong vegetable stock in a small amount of water. Peel, wash and cut vegetables into smaller pieces, put them into boiling water, add a bay leaf and allspice, and bring to the boil over a high heat. Turn the heat down and cook the vegetables until tender. Put the washed tomatoes, cut into smaller pieces, into a second pot. Add a clove of garlic strained through a garlic press and Provençal herbs, cook covered for about 15 minutes, stirring from time to time and checking to see if the tomatoes are tender. Strain the cooked tomatoes through a sieve and mix with the strained vegetable broth. If you like creamy soups, you can blend the cooked soup vegetables (without leek) and mix with tomato stock. Season to taste, i.e. with a tbsp of lemon juice if the tomatoes are sweet, or with a tbsp of honey if sour, powdered paprika, salt, pepper and herbs.

You can serve this soup with pasta, rice or bread croutons, and garnish with scraps of Parmesan cheese, basil leaves or a spiral of cream. The soup will be much more tasty, but also more calorific, if you cook the tomatoes in butter.

½ litre of fermented beet base or
    beetroot soup concentrate

½ litre of cream

½ litre of natural yoghurt

2 tbsp of finely chopped chives

1 cucumber

1 bunch of radishes

2 tbsp of finely chopped leaves of
    young beet greens

2 tbsp of lemon juice

salt, sugar, white pepper

Seasonal cold soup

Blend fermented beet base with cream and yoghurt. Add finely chopped vegetables: a washed and peeled green cucumber, radishes and young beet greens. Season to taste with salt, pepper, sugar and lemon juice. You can make the cold soup with a clove of garlic strained through a garlic press, finely chopped dill or a pinch of coriander, adding your favourite seasonal vegetables. The soup should be set aside for a couple of hours so that the ingredients blend well. It is served chilled from the fridge with hard-boiled eggs, cut into pieces, accompanied by cold roast veal, shrimps or crayfish.

This seasonal cold soup can also be made on the basis of sour milk or yoghurt without cream. You can find the recipe for fermented beet base on page 49.

Tripe

1 kg of tripe
soup vegetables
1 tbsp of butter
1 vegetable stock cube
1 tsp of marjoram
1 clove of garlic
1 bay leaf
a few seeds of allspice
salt, pepper
a pinch of nutmeg

Clean tripe thoroughly, put into boiling water and cook for 15 minutes. Pour out the water, cover the tripe again with boiling water and cook over a low heat, adding soup vegetables, a bay leaf and allspice. The stock will be stronger if you add a stock cube (MSG-free). Cut the cooked trip into small pieces and place in the soup with the chopped vegetables. You can also cut raw vegetables into matchsticks, fry in a small amount of fat and add them to the tripe, cooked in stock. The key when it comes to this soup is adding flavour with marjoram, nutmeg, salt, pepper, a clove of garlic strained through a garlic press and a tsp of butter. The recipe for tripe used to be carefully guarded. It was seasoned with a roux (a tbsp of flour browned in a tbsp of butter), finely chopped, browned onion and a glass of dry white wine. Marjoram, nutmeg, pepper and salt are a must when seasoning this dish, but you can also add thyme, powdered ginger and chilli pepper.

The tripe will be even more tasty if the dish is prepared a couple of hours before the meal. You can serve it with all kinds of side dishes, beginning with Parmesan cheese and ending with potato croquettes or meatballs made from minced meat or liver.

Soup from fresh mushrooms

Mushrooms have been a strong point of Polish cuisine for a long time, served in meat sauces, with groats and cakes, as an ingredient intensifying the flavour of a given dish, and as a flavouring for soups (e.g. borscht). Mushrooms are also added to bigos and cabbage served at the Christmas Eve supper. Served as a separate dish, stewed or fried in a coating, mushrooms have become a permanent fixture in the treasury of our cuisine.

½ kg of fresh mushrooms
  (chanterelles, oyster or
  champignons)

  soup vegetables

1 onion

1 tbsp of butter

4 potatoes

½ tsp of marjoram

1 tsp of lemon juice

1 tbsp of fresh herbs
  to garnish

1 bay leaf

  a few seeds of allspice

  salt, pepper, sugar

Cook vegetable stock with a few seeds of allspice, pepper and a bay leaf. Add a vegetable stock cube if you want to make it stronger. Melt a tbsp of butter in a frying pan and stir-fry finely chopped onion and thoroughly cleaned, washed mushrooms cut into small pieces. Season with salt, pepper and fry for a couple of minutes, then add to the vegetable broth. Put the potatoes (peeled, washed and cut into small pieces) into the boiling stock and cook together for 15 minutes. Before serving, season to taste with salt, pepper, marjoram, lemon juice and, optionally, a pinch of sugar. Once in bowls, sprinkle with your favourite herbs. The soup can be enhanced with cream, but you have to temper it first, i.e. mix it with a little bit of hot stock first.

Fish soup with dumplings

1 kg of fish fillets, preferably various kinds

1 tbsp of butter

1 onion

1 clove of garlic

1 vegetable stock cube

½ tsp of thyme

1 tbsp of lemon juice

2 tbsp of cream

salt, pepper, sugar

tiny home-made dumplings formed with a spoon or vermicelli

Heat butter in a frying pan and fry finely chopped onion for a couple of minutes. Prepare vegetable broth with a bay leaf and allspice, or dissolve an organic vegetable stock cube in boiling water. Place the onion in it with the cleaned and rinsed fish. After 20 minutes of cooking add a clove of garlic strained through a garlic press, thyme, lemon juice, and season with salt and pepper to taste. Strain the whole dish through a sieve and add cream.

Dumplings:

1 glass of flour

½ glass of milk

1 egg

a pinch of salt

1 tbsp of melted butter

Mix flour with milk, salt, a yolk and butter. Blend with egg whites whipped to a froth. Bring a large amount of water to the boil in a big pot (so that the dumplings have enough room) and heat a ablespoontbspbsp in boiling water. Scoop bits of dough onto the end of a tablespoontbsptbsp and put into the boiling water. The dough should be firm but fluffy. When they float on the surface, cover with a lid for a minute, and then delicately scoop out with a strainer.

Cabbage soup

soup vegetables

½ kg of sour cabbage

1 bay leaf

a few seeds of allspice

1 tbsp of butter

1 onion

150 g of smoked bacon or sausage

¼ tsp of ground cumin

½ tsp of marjoram

2 dried mushrooms

salt, pepper, sugar

Put the peeled and washed soup vegetables into boiling water together with bay leaf, allspice, washed dried mushrooms and chopped sour cabbage. Cook over a low heat for about half an hour. Melt the butter in a frying pan, peel and finely chop onion, fry it, and add cumin, marjoram, salt and pepper. Put into the soup. If you like thick soups, add a roux made from a tbsp of butter and a tbsp of browned flour. Cut the sausage or smoked bacon into smaller pieces, fry in a frying pan and add to the soup, removing some melted fat with a strainer. Take out the vegetables from the soup, put aside or cut into smaller pieces and throw them back in. Season the dish to taste with salt, pepper and a pinch of sugar. If the cabbage is not very sour, you can enhance the flavour by adding lemon juice. You can serve the soup with potatoes, but cook them separately because the juice from fermented cabbage would make them hard and tasteless if thrown into the soup. This soup, called kwaśnica, is popular in the mountains. Usually its basis is meat stock, made from a piece of goose, or ribs.

Barley soup

Put the rinsed piece of meat into two litres of boiling water, with a bay leaf, allspice, rinsed barley groats (the best way is to pour them into a cup and cover with cold water so that the husks and other impurities float to the surface), a dried mushroom and an MSG-free stock cube. When the meat becomes a little tender (it takes about an hour for veal and much shorter in the case of fowl), put the washed and cleaned soup vegetables into the pot. Cook for about half an hour and add peeled potatoes, washed and cut into cubes. Cook for 20 minutes more. At the end add spices: garlic, marjoram, oregano, salt and pepper. Cut the meat and vegetables from the soup into cubes before serving, and sprinkle the plates with finely chopped parsley leaves.

Depending on the region, the barley soup can have more dried mushrooms, which alter its colour and flavour, or browned onion and smoked bacon scratchings. You can also add a tbsp of cream or a yolk, although I like it thick and bright in colour.

You can also make barley soup using millet groats.

200 g of chicken or veal

2 heaped tbsp of pearl barley groats

soup vegetables

1 cube of vegetable stock

1 bay leaf

a few seeds of allspice

1 clove of garlic

½ tsp of marjoram

½ tsp of oregano

1 dried mushroom

4 potatoes

1 tsp of finely chopped parsley leaves

salt, white pepper

Porcini mushroom soup with short pasta

(called łazanki in Polish)

a dozen or so dried
mushrooms

1 tbsp of butter

1 onion

1 vegetable stock cube or
freshly cooked vegetable
stock

2 tbsp of cream

1 tbsp of lemon juice

½ tsp of marjoram

1 bay leaf

a few seeds of allspice

salt, pepper and sugar

Wash the mushrooms, cover them with warm, boiled water and leave overnight to soak. Put the mushrooms cut into slices into a pot, pour in the water left from soaking, add a cube of vegetable stock (or peeled and washed soup vegetables), a bay leaf and allspice, and cook for about an hour until tender. When cooking add finely chopped onion, cooked in butter (which is not recommended if you want to make clear soup for the Christmas Eve supper). Season with salt, pepper and marjoram. Temper cream and pour into the soup after removing from the heat, or leave as a clear stock. Season to taste with a tbsp of lemon juice or ¼ glass of dry white wine and a pinch of sugar. Serve with short pasta.

A porcini soup from fresh mushrooms is made from the mushrooms stewed in butter with onion and mixing them with a vegetable stock and cream. Short pasta should be cooked separately, but add a little water left from cooking to the soup, if you want it thick.

Short pasta:

1 glass of flour

1 egg

2 tbsp of hot milk

a pinch of salt

Mix the ingredients, knead the dough, roll it on a work surface sprinkled with flour, cut. Boil in a large amount of salted water. Scoop them out with a strainer when they float to the surface.

Cucumber soup

Put the rinsed piece of meat, a bay leaf and allspice into boiling water, together with peeled and washed soup vegetables, add salt. Cook for about an hour, depending on the type of meat. Add the peeled potatoes, washed and cut into cubes, cook for 20 minutes, then add the peeled pickles grated using a large-hole grater, together with the juice. Heat the butter in a frying pan, stir-fry the very finely chopped onion and garlic, and after a short while add the peeled fresh cucumber, cut into quarters. Cook for 5 minutes and put everything into the soup. Season with salt, pepper and marjoram. Cut the soup vegetables and meat into smaller pieces. Sprinkle with finely chopped parsley leaves when in bowls.

200 g of white meat (chicken, turkey or veal)

250 g of pickled cucumbers

1 fresh cucumber

1 tbsp of clarified butter

soup vegetables

4 potatoes

1 clove of garlic

1 tbsp of butter

1 bay leaf

a few seeds of allspice

½ tsp of marjoram

1 tsp of finely chopped parsley leaves

salt, pepper, sugar

½ a chicken

½ kg of beef for stock, or shin

¼ head of savoy cabbage

   soup vegetables

1 bay leaf

   a few seeds of allspice

   a few seeds of pepper

1 clove of garlic

1 tsp of ginger

1 tbsp of lemon rind, thinly
   peeled and scalded

1 onion

2 cloves

Traditional broth

Boil 2 litres of water in a large pot. Brown the peeled onion evenly in a dry and heated frying pan, remove from the pan and stick the cloves into it. Put two pieces of meat into the boiling water (chicken and beef), and add soup vegetables, with lots of carrots, peeled, washed and cut into slightly smaller pieces. Add a bay leaf, allspice, pepper, the onion with cloves and a halved clove of garlic. To make sure the broth is tasty, cook it for a long time over a low heat. When the meat is tender, add a piece of savoy or white cabbage, slices of ginger and thinly peeled lemon rind. Season to taste with salt and pepper and set aside, so that the flavours blend together. This thick broth is served with pasta or meatballs. It will be all the more delicious and glutinous if you add giblets. An easy solution to remove excess fat formed on the surface of the broth is to keep it in the fridge. It is worth storing it and using it as an addition to pasta sauce, for instance.

Beef from the stock is served in a ring of vegetables cooked in the broth.

Borscht

Peel the washed beets and cut them into slices and then put into a large pot. Peel, wash and cut the soup vegetables into smaller pieces, add to beets, following with allspice, a bay leaf, as well as washed and dried mushrooms. Cover with water (so that the vegetables are submerged) and cook over a high heat, bringing the soup to the boil. Reduce the heat and cook for an hour and a half. Strain the stock, season with lemon juice, oregano, marjoram, cloves of garlic cut in half, a tbsp of honey, salt and pepper. Set aside so that the ingredients blend together well and bring to the boil before serving.

Clear borscht can be served in many ways: with an egg, ravioli, French pastry dumplings or various kinds of patties, as well as with potatoes and beans seasoned with onion or smoked bacon.

Borscht can also be prepared from beets pickled beforehand. Peel the washed beets, cut them into pieces, cover with water, add the crust of wholemeal bread and two cloves of garlic. Leave in a warm place for a week. Remove the mould, if any, and mix with thick vegetable or meat stock, keeping in mind that you cannot bring to the boil the borscht made on a fermented beet base (it would lose its colour and flavour).

The same ingredients can be used to make beet cream soup. All you have to do is blend some of the vegetables, mix them with the stock and season to taste.

This national soup of ours, boasting a long tradition, will taste slightly different if you add a piece of smoked bacon.

1 kg of beets
soup vegetables
1 bay leaf
a few seeds of allspice
a few dried mushrooms
2 cloves of garlic
a pinch of marjoram
a pinch of oregano
½ cup of lemon juice
1 tbsp of honey
salt and pepper

Sour soup

100 g of bacon or sausage
  (e.g. raw sausage)

1 bottle of fermented rye
  flour

1 litre of vegetable stock
  (preferably from soup
  vegetables)

1 bay leaf

  a few seeds of allspice

1 dried mushroom

1 clove of garlic

1 tbsp of grated horseradish

4 potatoes

2 eggs

½ tsp of marjoram

1 tbsp of lemon juice

  salt, pepper and sugar

This dates back further than the borscht.

Cut the lean bacon or sausage into cubes and fry in a frying pan. Add raw sausage to the boiling soup.

Put the fried bacon or sausage into the pot with the boiling vegetable stock, together with the potatoes cut into cubes, a crushed dried mushroom, season with salt and pepper, a bay leaf and allspice and cook for 20 minutes. Season with marjoram, a clove of garlic strained through a garlic press, pour in well stirred sour soup, add a tbsp of horseradish, lemon juice and sugar or, better yet, a tbsp of honey. Mix together, heat but don't bring to the boil. Hard-boil eggs, cool, shell and cut them into quarters. Place the eggs in broth cups (you can cook raw sausage and add it to the soup), pour the sour soup in. You can also season the soup with two tbsp of cream and sprinkle with fresh herbs.

Recipe for leavening: cover two glasses of wholemeal rye flour with boiling water to obtain a thin dough. When it cools, add tepid water and crust from wholemeal bread. Set aside for 3 days in a warm place in a glass jar, covered with gauze. You can store it for up to two weeks in corked bottles.

You can use sour soup to make a dish from regional cuisine called "zalewajka" (traditional potato soup with rye flour, cream and garlic). It's main ingredient is potatoes cut into cubes. Add pork fat or bacon scratchings.

1 kg of sauerkraut

½ kg of fresh cabbage

½ kg of smoked bacon

  a few dried mushrooms

2 onions

2 tbsp of olive oil

200 g of dried plums

1 tbsp of plum jam

½ glass of mead

1 tbsp of honey

1 tsp of ground cumin

2 bay leaves

½ tsp of powdered marjoram

  salt, pepper

Bigos

In its simplest form bigos can be made with smoked bacon cut into cubes, but it will be really delicious if you add to the stewed cabbage a variety of flavours, i.e. roasted meats, smoked bacon and sausage.

Soak the mushrooms (if dried whole, they need to be soaked for a couple of hours; for mushrooms in thin slices one hour will be enough), cook in the soaking water and set aside. Shred the fresh cabbage thoroughly, add salt and chopped sauerkraut. Fry two finely chopped large onions in olive oil, add salt. Add both types of cabbage, mushrooms with the stock in which they were cooked, bay leaves and enough boiling water (or even better a vegetable stock) to cover the cabbage.

Cook the cabbage over a low heat with the lid slid off to leave room for steam to escape, adding various kinds of roasted meats and sausages cut into cubes, gravy or at the very least smoked bacon stir-fried in a frying pan and cut into pieces. Add the dried plums soaked beforehand (cut, pitted), a tbsp of plum jam and various spices, like juniper, marjoram and cumin, mead (in the old days, it was recommended to add Madeira wine, but half a glass of dry red wine will do), honey, salt and pepper. Cook the dish over a low heat for another thirty minutes and put aside, so that the ingredients blend well together. It tastes best reheated.

Plum jam can be replaced with tomato paste, and you can add variety to the whole dish with a tbsp of grated horseradish and cloves of garlic strained through a garlic press.

Bigos is our national dish, which I have tasted in a sweet-flavoured version with raisins, as well as in a dry-flavoured version with peeled tomatoes. It can be stored in the fridge for quite a long time. After reheating it's difficult to tell the ingredients apart, but the taste of the cabbage is splendid.

Cabbage, served in Polish homes at the Christmas Eve supper, is a dish which does not include any meat. The other ingredients remain the same and are a part of a traditional family recipe. You can mix this cabbage with peas cooked until tender and seasoned with a roux from a tbsp of butter and a tbsp of flour.

In the pots warmed the bigos; mere words cannot tell
Of its wondrous taste, colour and marvellous smell.
One can hear the words buzz, and the rhymes ebb and flow,
But its content no city digestion can know.
To appreciate the Lithuanian folksong and folk food,
You need health, live on land, and be back from the wood.

Without these, still a dish of no mediocre worth
Is bigos, made from legumes, best grown in the earth;
Pickled cabbage comes foremost, and properly chopped,
Which itself, is the saying, will in ones mouth hop;
In the boiler enclosed, with its moist bosom shields
Choicest morsels of meat raised on greenest of fields;
Then it simmers, till fire has extracted each drop
Of live juice, and the liquid boils over the top,
And the heady aroma wafts gently afar.

Now the bigos is ready.

Adam Mickiewicz "Pan Tadeusz"
Translated by Marcel Weyland

Red cabbage with apples and raisins

½ kg of red cabbage

1 wine-flavoured apple

a handful of raisins

1 onion

2 tbsp of olive oil

3 tbsp of lemon juice

1 tsp of honey

salt, pepper

Soak the raisins in a small amount of hot water. Wash the cabbage with outer leaves removed and shred thoroughly. Heat oil in a saucepan, stir-fry finely chopped onion, add cabbage and three tbsp of hot water or dry red wine, cover and cook for a couple of minutes over a low heat, until the cabbage is no longer raw. Add a fresh apple, cut into small pieces, and raisins, season to taste with salt, pepper and honey, and mix together. Remove from the heat, season with lemon juice to give the cabbage a wonderful colour, and put into a serving dish.

You can use the same ingredients to make a salad from the cabbage. First blanch finely shredded cabbage, i.e. steep it in boiling water, rinse with cold water, drain, mix with lemon juice, add finely chopped fresh onion, apples and raisins, season with salt, pepper, honey and oil.

Baked beans in tomato sauce

The best choice for this dish is fresh, young butter beans. If you are using dried beans, you have to soak them overnight. Cook until tender over a low heat adding vegetable stock cubes and a tsp of olive oil, so that the skin doesn't break. The beans need to be covered with cooking water, and you shouldn't pour out any of it, as after adding the remaining ingredients it will transform into a thick sauce. Fry the finely chopped onion in a tbsp of olive oil heated in a frying pan, add to beans, followed by a small can of tomato concentrate and a can of whole peeled tomatoes. Of course, you can use fresh, peeled tomatoes. Mix all the ingredients together, heat them and begin composing the flavour, i.e. season the dish with salt, pepper, marjoram, ground allspice, lemon juice, honey, favourite herbs, such as basil and ground cumin or garlic. If the dish is too thick, thin it down with the stock. If it's too watery, boil it uncovered for a little longer over a low heat, so that some of the liquid evaporates. This delicious dish can be served for a couple of days in a row (if stored in the fridge).

You will get the best results with this recipe if you add many kinds of stewed, roasted or cooked meats.

1 kg of butter beans

2 vegetable stock cubes

2 large onions

½ kg of smoked meat (bacon and sausage)

2 tbsp of olive oil

1 can of whole tomatoes, peele

1 small jar of tomato concentr

4 tbsp of spicy ketchup

1 tsp of sweet pepper

1 tsp of marjoram

1 tsp of powdered basil

½ tsp of ground allspice

2 tbsp of lemon juice

2 tbsp of honey

1 bay leaf

salt, pepper

½ kg of potatoes

1 courgette

1 onion

1 tbsp of clarified butter

1 carrot

1 clove of garlic

200 ml of 12% fat cream (this
ingredient is not necessary)

1 tbsp of Provençal herbs

a pinch of nutmeg

1 tbsp of olive oil for the mould

salt, pepper

Baked vegetables

Boil and slightly cool potatoes in their skins, peel them and cut into slices. Chop the onion finely. You can fry it in butter, adding salt and pepper, but you can use fresh onion as well. Cut the washed courgette and peeled carrot into slices. Spread the surface of a mould with olive oil or your favourite oil. Next, arrange in the shape of roof-tiling: a slice of potato, courgette, onion and carrot, alternately. Sprinkle with Provençal herbs and a pinch of nutmeg. Spread a clove of garlic strained through a garlic press over it and sprinkle with olive oil. Cover the mould with foil and put into a heated oven. Bake for about 20 minutes, remove foil so that the vegetables brown a little bit, and bake for a few minutes more. If you pour some cream over the dish, the vegetables will be crunchy and silky, but this ingredient is optional. You can pick and choose your vegetables, adding all kinds of cheese, and add some variety with olives, nuts or seeds.

Washed, young potatoes are delicious, arranged in a mould and sprinkled with finely chopped rosemary needles. It's also a good idea to add a few peeled cloves of garlic, sprinkle the dish with olive oil and coarse sea salt, and place in a preheated oven for 45 minutes, covering with foil at the beginning, so that they don't brown too much. Raw potatoes require longer baking, but they will be subtly crispy. Long baking will also give the garlic a delicate sweet flavour. The best solution is to bake whole cloves, preferably wrapped in foil.

$\mathcal{S}$tewed mushrooms

Fry finely chopped onion with salt until transparent, add peeled mushrooms (washed, drained and cut into small pieces), cover and stew over a low heat for 10-15 minutes. If the mushrooms produce a lot of sauce, uncover the lid a little bit and let some of it evaporate. Add cream and stir. Heavy cream can be added directly to the mushrooms, but if you are using lighter cream, you have to temper it first, i.e. mix it with a tbsp of the hot mushroom sauce first and stew together for a while longer until the sauce thickens. Season to taste with salt, pepper and a pinch of dried marjoram. If you like your sauce thick, mix cream with a tbsp of flour.

You can finish it off with two raw eggs, mixed with a tbsp of finely chopped chives or parsley leaves.

Honey mushrooms and morels need to be parboiled first.

½ kg of fresh mushrooms

1 large onion

100 ml of cream

a pinch of marjoram

salt, pepper

Potato and cheese pierogi

Dough:

2 glasses of flour

1 egg

2 tbsp of olive oil

⅓ glass of hot water

a pinch of salt

Stuffing:

4 large potatoes

1 onion

1 tbsp of butter

150 g of smooth cottage cheese

salt, pepper

a few mint leaves

a pinch of herbs (marjoram, oregano)

Peel the potatoes, wash them and cut into small pieces. Put them into boiling water for about 20 minutes and add salt towards the end. Drain off and set aside to cool a little. To make the best pierogi you need freshly made stuffing. Fry finely chopped onion in heated butter, add salt and herbs.

I like to make my work simpler by mashing warm potatoes and cheese into a silky pulp using a potato masher with holes. Then I add the onion and herbs, mix together and season the stuffing to taste with salt and white pepper. If you boil potatoes earlier, you have to mash them while still warm, to make sure you get a smooth pulp. Mix sifted flour with a whole, raw egg, a pinch of salt and olive oil or melted butter. This will make the dough more springy and you'll be able to roll it up into a thin layer. Adding hot water will do the trick, too. Once kneaded, move it onto a pastry board or a work surface sprinkled with flour. After some kneading, when it stops absorbing flour and doesn't stick to your hands (don't make it too thick, as it will be hard to roll it up), divide it into small pieces and roll up, sprinkling a rolling pin with flour and making sure the dough doesn't stick to the surface. Cut circles out of it using a glass of the right size, place stuffing on it and tightly seal the edges with less flour. You put the pierogi into salted boiling water and scoop them out with a strainer once they float on the surface. You should pour a tbsp of oil into the boiling water so that the pierogi don't stick together. If you are not serving them at once, spread a thin layer of olive oil over the serving dish as well.

You can add a finely chopped clove of garlic or a pinch of powdered garlic to the stuffing, while replacing cottage cheese with feta cheese.

Pierogi are a popular dish, and they are served in more and more gastronomic outlets with a multitude of stuffing flavours:

- minced meat, cooked or stewed beforehand, mixed with finely chopped onion, fried in butter and spices;
- buckwheat cooked beforehand, mixed with finely chopped onion, fried in butter and smoked bacon scratchings;
- boiled potatoes mixed with boiled green peas and stewed onion with spices;
- grated, raw potatoes, thoroughly strained, also with the addition of stewed onion and scratchings;
- stewed, finely chopped mushrooms with onion (the stuffing should be quite thick, so that the edges of the dough don't come undone);
- sauerkraut stewed with onion and mushrooms or raw cabbage, stewed with onion and spices;
- cheese mixed with finely chopped olives or stewed vegetables;
- boiled broccoli mixed with cottage cheese, a clove of garlic strained through a press, an egg and breadcrumbs;

- spinach fried in butter, mixed with grated Parmesan cheese, cottage cheese and an egg;
- boiled and peeled broad beans, mixed with cooked onion and seasoned to taste with dill and garlic;
- hard-boiled eggs, finely chopped and mixed with onion, fried in butter, finely chopped parsley leaves or dill and spices;
- finely crumbled nuts, mixed with cottage cheese, fresh basil, garlic and an egg;
- finely crumbled nuts, cottage cheese, raisins and a yolk stirred with sugar;
- fruit (strawberries, pitted plums, bilberries mixed with sugar);
- poppy seeds ground twice, mixed with raisins, honey and a pinch of powdered cinnamon. The stuffing will be thicker if you mix it with a raw egg.

Lithuanian dumplings

Stuffing:

300 g of tenderloin (finely
    chopped or minced)

1 onion

1 tbsp of olive oil

1 tbsp of grated marjoram

    salt, pepper

Dough:

¼ kg of flour

2 eggs

¼ glass of hot water

1 tbsp of olive oil

    a pinch of salt

1 vegetable stock cube

Knead springy dough. Make the stuffing by mixing raw meat, onion cooked in broth and blended (or finely chopped and stewed in oil) with salt, pepper and marjoram.

Roll up the dough on a work surface sprinkled with flour, cut circles using a wine glass or a regular glass (the smaller the better). Place them in the cup of your hand, add stuffing and seal the ends tightly. The stuffing will grow in volume during cooking, so be sure not to put too much inside.

Put dumplings in boiling broth (preferably from beef, but you can also dissolve a vegetable stock cube in boiling water) and after a few minutes when they float on the surface scoop them out with a strainer. You can serve them with the broth or with butter poured over, as well as with a cream sauce with garlic.

They taste delicious with the stuffing made from tenderloin and lamb in equal proportions.

Originally the stuffing was made from mutton.

Ravioli

Dough:

2 glasses of flour

2 eggs

½ glass of hot water

1 tbsp of olive oil

a pinch of salt

Stuffing:

100 g of dried mushrooms

1 onion

1 tbsp of butter

a pinch of marjoram

salt, pepper

Rinse the mushrooms and soak in a small amount of water. Whole mushroom caps need to be soaked overnight, while ones cut into slices will only take an hour to be ready. Boil them in the water left from soaking. Once cool, rinse, cut finely (keep the stock for a soup or a sauce) and add finely chopped onion, fried in butter. Season to taste with salt, pepper and marjoram, mix together and leave aside while making the dough.

Knead the flour, eggs, a pinch of salt, a tbsp of olive oil and hot water into a springy dough.

Roll it up and cut out squares, preferably with 4-cm wide sides. Place stuffing on one half, first seal them into triangles, and then join the edges together. Put into salted boiling water, boil for a few minutes, and after they float on the surface, delicately scoop out with a strainer. They taste best with borscht served at the Christmas Eve supper or a mushroom soup.

The dough can also be prepared from 25 g of flour, 1 egg, 1 tbsp of oil and 1 boiled potato. If the stuffing is too thin, add a tbsp of breadcrumbs. A raw egg will do the trick, too.

Potato dumplings

Boil the peeled potatoes, adding salt towards the end. Drain off the potatoes, cool them and mince or mash adding an egg, salt and flour with potato flour to make them glutinous. Flour will help blend the soft dough together (the potato flour is not a necessary ingredient; potato dumplings can be made from wheat flour alone). You can also make them by combining wheat and spelt flour. Knead the soft dough and shape rolls about two centimetres thick on a pastry board sprinkled with flour. Flatten them slightly and cut diagonally into dumplings. Put them into boiling water and wait a few minutes before scooping them out with a strainer when they float to the surface. Boil them in patches in plenty of salted boiled water so that they don't stick together. You can add a tbsp of oil. The dumplings can be refried in a frying pan or in the oven and served with melted butter or other fat, with smoked bacon or onion scratchings. In autumn I make them from the pulp of a baked pumpkin.

½ kg of potatoes

1 glass of flour

1 tbsp of potato flour

1 egg

salt

Silesian dumplings

Peel the potatoes, wash them and boil, adding salt towards the end. Drain, cool slightly, mince, purée or mash, then mix with the two flours, salt and eggs. Knead into a soft, springy dough. Divide into a few pieces, make three-centimetre wide rolls, cut into three-centimetre strips and give them an oval shape using your hands. Make a hole in the centre so that they boil faster and more evenly and the sauce clings to the dumplings more easily. Boil in salted water for a couple of minutes after they float to the surface. Scoop out with a strainer and serve with your favourite sauce, or pour fat and browned salted onion over the dish.

You can use the same dough to make larger dumplings with stuffing. They can be prepared with minced poultry meat,, mixed with stewed onion and spices. Another way to make the dumplings is to mix boiled potatoes with a little grated potato, drained off from the watery juice.

1 kg potatoes

1½ glasses of wheat flour

½ glass of potato flour

2 eggs

salt

Potato plum-dumplings

½ kg of ripe plums

1 kg potatoes

1 glass of flour

2 eggs

50 g of butter

1 tbsp of breadcrumbs

salt, pepper

Wash the peeled potatoes and boil, adding salt towards the end. Drain, cool slightly, mince, strain or mash, then mix with salt, eggs and flour. You can add a tbsp of potato flour, knead to a soft but compact dough, make a roll with a diameter one centimetre larger than that of the plums, cut into dumplings. Cut the washed and dried plums in half and pit them. Place a dumpling in the palm of your hand, top with a plum and close it, sealing the dough and shaping the dumplings with your hands. Put into salted boiling water and scoop out a few minutes after they float on the surface. Take out with a strainer. Serve hot with melted butter poured over with browned breadcrumbs (first brown breadcrumbs in a frying pan and only add butter later). If the plums are not sweet enough, you can serve sugar separately.

Potato plum-dumplings can be served sweet-flavoured with, e.g. strawberry stuffing, or salted with a stuffing from stewed mushrooms, finely chopped onion and spices or blanched spinach, finely chopped and mixed with grated cheese, breadcrumbs and a pressed clove of garlic.

Potato pie

Grate the peeled and washed potatoes on a grater and drain slightly. Fry the back bacon, cut into thin strips on a frying pan with finely chopped onion. Add to potatoes the whole raw egg and yoghurt, mix, combine with the bacon and onion, season to taste with salt, pepper and finely chopped leaves of fresh sage. Spread the mould with fat, put the dish in and bake for about an hour in a preheated oven.

The dish will be delicious if you add finely chopped roast or stewed mushrooms.

Similar hash browns can be prepared from cooked buckwheat groats.

1 kg of potatoes

1 egg

1 tbsp of Greek or other yoghurt of similar consistency

½ kg of smoked back bacon

a few leaves of fresh sage

salt, pepper

fat for a mould

Potato cakes

1 kg of potatoes

1 onion (optional)

3 heaped tbsp of wholemeal flour

2 eggs

1 tsp of salt

   olive oil or favourite cooking oil

   pepper

   cream

Peel the potatoes and grate them coarsely, the same as the onion, set aside for a while, slightly drain, collecting the juice and pouring out the watery part. Add thick starch from the bottom to the potato pulp. Mix with flour, eggs and salt. Heat quite a bit of fat to a high temperature. Place thin dough with a tbsp onto the frying pan, shaping cakes. When browned, turn over. Serve hot with fat cream, chanterelle mushrooms stewed in cream, caviar or other additions. Potato cakes with sugar are also popular, in which case the onion is not necessary. An interesting version of this recipe is made by adding all kinds of scratchings, e.g. from pork fat or bacon, as well as finely chopped parsley leaves or cottage cheese.

Potato dumplings

Boil the peeled potatoes until tender, adding salt towards the end. Drain and mash with the cheese. Mix with the eggs and flour. Fry the finely chopped onion in butter, season with salt and pepper. Combine with the potato-cheese pulp, season to taste with salt and marjoram, and blend with the almond flakes.

Bring salted water to the boil. First heat a tbsp in boiling water. Scoop dough with the tip of the tbsp and put it into the boiling water. The dumplings are ready a few minutes after they float to the surface. You can pour melted butter over them, sprinkle with smoked bacon scratchings or serve with a sauce.

If you add 2 tbsp of finely chopped ham to the pulp, the dumplings will have a very strong flavour. If you use a greater with large holes to grate an apple, it will also change the character of the dish, and so will blanched and finely chopped spinach.

½ kg of potatoes

300 g of cottage cheese

1 onion

1 tbsp of clarified butter

2 eggs

½ glass of flour

   a handful of almond flake:

1 tsp of marjoram

   salt, pepper

Short pasta (łazanki) with cabbage and mushrooms

Dough:

2 glasses of flour

1 egg

1 boiled potato

3 tbsp of olive oil

Stuffing:

250 g of fresh mushrooms

½ of medium savoy or white cabbage

2 onions

1 tbsp of breadcrumbs

1 tsp of marjoram

1 tbsp of lemon juice

1 tbsp of finely chopped parsley leaves

salt, pepper, sugar

Add one boiled potato to sifted flour, blend with a whole raw egg and two tbsp of olive oil. Gradually add boiled, warm water, kneading the thin dough constantly. Roll up the well kneaded, springy dough on a pastry board sprinkled with flour, slightly dry, cut into strips, sprinkle with flour and cut diagonally into short pasta shapes. Boil in water, adding a tbsp of oil to prevent them from sticking together.

Fry finely chopped onion in two tbsp of fat, add the cleaned, washed mushrooms cut into small pieces, season to taste with salt and pepper and cook covered for 15 minutes over a low heat. Cut the cabbage into quarters, boil in water with salt and sugar, drain when tender, cut into small pieces, and mix with marjoram and lemon juice. Combine the short pasta, mushrooms and cabbage, serving immediately or arranging in layers in a buttered heat-resistant dish. Pour a little melted butter over it, sprinkle with breadcrumbs and cook until golden brown in the oven. Sprinkle with finely chopped parsley leaves, dill or chives before serving.

You can also mix short pasta with sauerkraut, but first boil it until tender with a glass of thick stock, evaporate, i.e. cook without a lid, seasoning to taste with garlic and herbs as well as salt and pepper. Other ingredients remain unchanged.

Cottage cheese dumplings

Blend the cottage cheese with a tbsp of butter, cream, a pinch of salt, sugar, eggs and flour. You can add the yolks first, finishing with the egg whites whipped to a froth. Knead thin dough carefully, put it on a pastry board or a clean work surface sprinkled with flour, and shape rolls with a diameter of about 2 cm. Flatten them a little – you can cut a chequered pattern with a knife and cut diagonally so that the dumplings have a uniform shape. Put them into salted boiling water and carefully scoop out with a strainer once they float to the surface. Pour butter with browned breadcrumbs over them. To prevent the breadcrumbs from absorbing too much fat, first brown them in a dry frying pan and add butter later. You can serve curd cheese dumplings with cream, as well as fruit, nuts, seeds and raisins.

If the cheese is smooth, you don't need cream.

½ kg of cottage cheese

2 eggs

2 tbsp of cream

1 glass of flour

100 g of butter

1 tbsp of breadcrumbs

salt, pepper

Buckwheat groats

It's best to buy light, un-roasted groats in organic food stores.

1 glass of buckwheat groats

2½ glasses of water

1 tsp of dried dill

   a few fenugreek seeds

1 vegetable stock cube

1 tbsp of butter

1 tbsp of olive oil

Melt the oil and butter in a pot, add the buckwheat and brown it for a couple of minutes. Make sure the buckwheat doesn't burn. Pour in cold water, add a vegetable stock cube, mix and boil covered for 20 minutes. Towards the end season with dry dill and fenugreek. Buckwheat tastes delicious when reheated, and it can also be a basis for croquettes.

Millet groats

Melt the olive oil and butter in a pot, fry the finely chopped onion and finely cut pepper (washed and pitted). Pour the groats into a sieve, rinse with cold water, drain, add to the onion and pepper, stir and cook together for a few minutes. Pour hot milk and hot water over it, mix together and boil covered over a low heat until tender (for more than half an hour). Towards the end add dried dill and stir together. When the groats are tender remove from the heat, add salt and cheese, season with pepper and stir. You can put the groats into a cup or some other mould, compact them a little and place portions of the aromatic groats onto a dish. Pour your favourite sauce over or serve as an addition to stewed meat or vegetables.

1 glass of millet groats
1½ glasses of water
1 glass of milk
1 tbsp of olive oil
1 tbsp of butter
1 tbsp of dried dill
1 onion
1 red pepper
2 tbsp of grated Parmesan cheese or some spicy Swiss cheese
salt, pepper

A groat and potato cake from Cracow

Peel, wash and boil the potatoes, drain and then mash them. Mix with the groats and raw yolks, season with dill, pepper and nutmeg. At the end add the egg whites whipped to a froth. Put into a buttered mould coated with breadcrumbs and place in a preheated oven for about 40 minutes.

1 kg of potatoes
½ glass of Cracow groats (or 1 tbsp more)
2 eggs
4 tbsp of butter
1 tbsp of dried dill
1 tbsp of breadcrumbs
1 tbsp of butter
a pinch of nutmeg
salt, pepper

600 g of sole or other white fish

250 g of grapes

1 glass of vegetable stock

1 tbsp of mustard

2 tbsp of cream

4 tbsp of dry white wine

2 tbsp of olive oil or other
vegetable oil

2 tbsp of flour

1 tbsp of butter

1 tsp of flour

a few sprigs of dill

salt, pepper

Fillets in a grape sauce

Wash the grapes, cut them in half and remove seeds.

Divide the rinsed and drained fillets into pieces, add salt, sprinkle with pepper, coat in flour, and fry until golden in heated olive oil or your oil of choice, leaving on each side for a couple of minutes. Prepare the grape sauce in a small saucer, i.e. melt a tbsp of butter, brown a tsp of flour in it, add vegetable stock (you can dissolve a stock cube in boiling water) and boil over a low heat, until the sauce thickens, add cream, white wine and light mustard (preferably honey-flavoured). At the end add the grape halves without seeds and heat the whole dish for a few moments. Place the fried fillets on a serving dish, pour the sauce over and garnish with dill sprigs.

Fillets with onion and cream sauce

Rub the rinsed fillets with pepper, put into a pot, steep in the milk. Soften the finely chopped onion in oil, season with salt and pepper, add honey, fry for a bit together, and then add the balsamic vinegar, wine and cream, and season to taste with salt and pepper. Cook the fish in milk with vegetable stock cube (about 10 minutes over a low heat). Place in a saucepan with the sauce and heat together. Place the dish on a serving plate, and garnish with dill or other herbs and slices of lemon.

600 g of hake fillets
2 onions
2 tbsp of olive oil
2 tbsp of balsamic vinegar
4 tbsp of dry white wine
1 tbsp of light honey
4 tbsp of cream
2 glasses of milk
1 vegetable stock cube
1 lemon
a few sage leaves
a sprig of dill
salt, pepper

Fish balls in dill sauce

Mince the fillets in a grinder, soak the roll in a small amount of vegetable stock or milk. Soften the finely chopped onion in melted butter. Mix the fish, the pressed roll, fried onion and raw egg, season to taste with salt and pepper, and knead into a smooth pulp. Put the round fish balls into hot vegetable stock and boil over a low heat for about 20 minutes. Scoop out with a strainer, place on a serving dish and keep warm. Mix the cream with a little stock to temper it, pour into the stock left from boiling the fish balls, season to taste with ginger, garlic and pepper, bring to the boil, add finely chopped dill and pour over the fish balls.

600 g of fish fillets
1 onion
2 tbsp of butter
1 stale bread roll
1 glass of vegetable stock
1 egg
½ litre of vegetable stock (boiled from vegetables and spices or from a cube dissolved in boiling water)
1 small carton of thick cream
1 tsp of flour
1 tbsp of finely chopped fresh dill
a pinch of white pepper
a pinch of powdered ginger
a pinch of powdered garlic
salt

Cooked carp

Carp holds a prominent place in Polish cuisine due to the tradition of serving it at the Christmas Eve supper.

1 kg skinned fish

   soup vegetables

2 onions

1 glass of dry white wine

¼ kg of mushrooms

2 tbsp of butter

1 tbsp of flour

1 tbsp of lemon juice

   a few seeds of allspice

1 bay leaf

   a tbsp of finely chopped
   parsley leaves

   salt, pepper

Prepare a little thick stock from peeled and finely chopped soup vegetables, one onion and spices, cool slightly, and blend with the wine. Place the cleaned and rinsed carp in an oblong pot for cooking fish and steep it in the liquid. Cook covered over a low heat for half an hour. Melt the butter in a frying pan and fry the finely chopped second onion for a couple of minutes, then add the washed and cleaned mushrooms. After 10 minutes add salt, a tbsp of flour mixed with two tbsp of fish stock, season to taste with pepper and lemon juice and cook for a couple of minutes more until the sauce thickens. Take the fish out carefully and place it on a serving dish, garnish with mushrooms, pour the sauce over it and sprinkle with finely chopped parsley leaves.

Carp cooked according to this recipe can also be served in a béchamel sauce. Let the fish down in the stock. It should be divided into pieces and boned. Place it in a heat-resistant dish. Pour the sauce over it, top with cheese flakes and pieces of butter and bake in a preheated oven.

The recipe for the simplest béchamel sauce is to melt 2 tbsp of butter in a saucepan, brown 2 tbsp of flour in it and add a glass of milk. Keep it over a low heat for a couple of minutes, stirring constantly, and you will get a thick sauce, which goes well with all kinds of roasts. You can season it to taste with lemon peel, salt, the seeds of a green pepper, capers, herbs, a pinch of nutmeg, or a few tbsp of cream with a raw yolk. The sauce will be more interesting if you make it adding clarified butter mixed with milk used to boil an onion with one clove and a bay leaf.

Fried carp

Cut a cleaned and rinsed carp into pieces, add salt and set aside for half an hour. Melt the butter in a frying pan, coat each piece of fish in flour, then in egg, and then breadcrumbs. Fry on both sides until golden over a medium heat. You can cover it for a while so that the fish is fried through.

100 g of butter

2 eggs

2 tbsp of flour

3 tbsp of breadcrumbs

salt, pepper

Crucian carp or tench in cream

Skin the fish, cut the heads and tails off, rinse, and divide larger fish into smaller portions. Sprinkle with salt and flour, and fry in heated fat until brown, turning on both sides. Cover with a glass of vegetable stock (it can also be made from a vegetable stock cube dissolved in boiling water) and cook covered for 10 minutes over a low heat. Pour sour cream over, season to taste with pepper and cook for another 5 minutes, this time uncovered. Serve the fish with cream sauce, sprinkled with dill or parsley leaves.

1 kg of crucian carp or tench

1 tbsp of butter

1 tbsp of olive oil

3 tbsp of flour

½ glass of cream

1 glass of vegetable stock

2 tbsp of finely chopped dill or parsley leaves

salt, white pepper

Stuffed trout

Fry the finely chopped onion and mushrooms in a tbsp of olive oil, pour in the wine and cook for a while, then season to taste with salt and pepper, adding the breadcrumbs and stirring at the end. Stuff the rinsed, cleaned and dried fish (keep the heads, but remove eyes and gills), sew up, add a pinch of salt, coat in flour and fry in fat on both sides until golden. Put in a heat-resistant dish, sprinkle with herbs and olive oil and place in a preheated oven for 15 minutes. When you take it out, sprinkle the fish with a tbsp of grated Parmesan cheese.

You can stuff trout with raw, finely chopped onion with a sprig of parsley, or crushed almond flakes mixed with a tbsp of honey, a tbsp of olive oil and pepper.

4 small trouts (250 g each)

2 onions

3 mushrooms

3 tbsp of breadcrumbs

1 glass of dry white wine

½ glass of olive oil or oil of choice

1 tsp of thyme

1 tsp of basil

1 tsp of finely chopped parsley leaves

salt, pepper

1 kg of eel
¾ litre of lager
2 onions
2 cloves
1 tbsp of orange peel
1 glass of port wine
3 tbsp of cream
1 tbsp of flour
3 tbsp of finely chopped fresh dill
    salt, pepper

Eel in dill sauce

Skin the fish (the best way is to make a nick at the head, hang the fish and pull off the skin evenly), cut into pieces, add salt. Pour the beer over it in a saucepan, and add the finely chopped onions, cloves, lemon peel and port wine. Leave in a cool place for an hour, and then boil over a low heat for half an hour more. Put the fish in a heat-resistant dish. Strain the stock from cooking through a sieve, add cream mixed with flour and dill, and cook over a low heat until the sauce thickens, stirring all the time. Season to taste with salt and pepper. Pour the sauce over the fish, place in a preheated oven and bake for 10 minutes.

400 g of cod fillets
1 onion
300 g of sauerkraut
    a glass of vegetable stock
2 tbsp of olive oil
1 bay leaf
1 tbsp of finely chopped parsley
    half a tsp of Provençal herbs
    salt, pepper

Cod with sauerkraut

Brown the peeled and finely chopped onion in olive oil lightly, mix with the chopped sauerkraut, steep in a glass of vegetable stock (which can be prepared from a vegetable stock cube dissolved in boiling water) and cook until tender, adding a thoroughly crushed bay leaf, Provençal herbs and a pinch of pepper. Top with the rinsed and slightly salted fillets, cut into small pieces and cook covered over a low heat for about 15 minutes. Serve on sauerkraut and sprinkle with parsley leaves.

You will add variety to this dish if instead of using vegetable stock you add a few dried mushrooms to the cooking stock, or scalded and peeled potatoes. Another option is to coat the cod in flour and fry, and then place in a heat-resistant dish and roast with stewed sauerkraut. Top with smoked bacon, cut into very thin slices.

Zander roasted with chanterelle mushrooms

800 g of zander (pike-perch)

200 g of chanterelle mushrooms

2 onions

4 tbsp of butter

½ glass of cream

50 g of Swiss cheese

a pinch of marjoram

salt, pepper

Divide the cleaned and rinsed fish into fillets and then into smaller pieces. Add salt, place in a heat-resistant dish, pour two tbsp of melted butter over the fish, and place in a preheated oven for 15 minutes. Use the rest of the butter to fry the finely chopped onion, add mushrooms cut into small pieces and cook together, seasoning lightly with salt, pepper and marjoram. Take out the slightly roasted fish, place a layer of chanterelle mushrooms with onion on it, pour slightly salted cream over it, sprinkle with grated cheese and put back into the preheated oven for 15 minutes to brown the cheese.

You can roast zander with bay leaves and the peel of a scalded lemon, with dill and dry white wine, parsley leaves, almond flakes, or béchamel sauce with green pepper.

Roasted halibut

Divide the rinsed and drained fish into portions, then sprinkle with lemon juice and set aside in the fridge while making a vegetable blanket. Peel, wash and cut the vegetables into small pieces (without onion). Boil in a small amount of water with a bay leaf and allspice (for a dozen or so minutes). Drain, and keep the stock for other purposes. In a small bowl prepare a sauce from the tomato concentrate, ketchup, olive oil and white wine. Mix the vegetables with finely chopped onion and the sauce. Season to taste with salt, pepper and thyme. Place portions of fish in a heat-resistant dish, cover with vegetables in tomato sauce and put in a preheated oven for 30 minutes. If you prefer a sweet flavour, you can brown a handful of raisins in butter and garnish the fish with them after taking it out of the oven.

800 g of halibut
2 tbsp of lemon juice
2 carrots
1 parsley
a piece of celeriac
1 onion
1 bay leaf
a few seeds of allspice
2 tbsp of tomato concentrate
2 tbsp of spicy ketchup
2 tbsp of olive oil
½ glass of dry white wine
1 tbsp of thyme
salt, pepper

1 kg of pike

   a glass of vegetable stock

   a glass of dry white wine

1 bay leaf

   a few seeds of allspice

1 lemon

1 apple

   a handful of raisins

   a handful of fresh wholemeal bread without crust

   a pinch of cinnamon

2 cloves

   salt, pepper, sugar

Old Polish pike

Scale and fillet the fish, then rinse and drain, cut into portions, rub with salt and leave in the fridge for half an hour. In a pot mix the vegetable stock with wine, add a bay leaf and allspice, and bring to the boil. Put in portions of pike and cook until tender over a low heat. Take the fish out (keep warm) and add cloves, cinnamon, breadcrumbs, raisins, an apple peeled and cut into thin slices (without the core) and lemon, cut into thin half-slices. Season to taste with salt, pepper and sugar. Put the fish onto a serving plate and pour the sauce over it.

You can add a little lemon peel grated with a citrus zester and (once you remove it from the heat) also a tbsp of horseradish.

1 kg of vendace

½ glass of flour

½ glass of olive oil

Marinade:

1 onion

1 sprig of parsley

   a slice of celeriac

2 bay leaves

   a few seeds of allspice

2 cloves

½ glass of white vinegar

2 glasses of water

   a pinch of sugar

Marinated fried vendace

Clean and divide the vendace into portions. Then add salt, coat it in flour and fry until golden in very hot oil. Cut the peeled and washed vegetables into small pieces, cover with two glasses of water and boil over a low heat with the bay leaves and the spices for 20 minutes. At the end add salt, vinegar and a pinch of sugar. Steep the fish in cooled marinade and leave the dish in the fridge for a couple of hours.

2 kg of roast beef

1 lemon

1 onion

2 carrots

a slice of celeriac

1 parsley

a few seeds of allspice

a few juniper berries

2 cloves

1 clove of garlic

1 bay leaf

½ tsp of ginger

salt, pepper

Marinated beef

Put the rinsed and drained meat into a stoneware pot, and add the chopped onion and soup vegetables grated using a large hole grater. Cover them with a hot marinade made from red wine, juice squeezed from a lemon, a bay leaf, a sliced clove of garlic, allspice, crushed cloves, finely sliced fresh ginger and ground berries of juniper. (You can also add a few dried plums). The meat should marinate for two days (you should check on it and turn it from side to side). Drain it, add a pinch of salt and sprinkle with pepper. Place it in a roasting tin with fat and put in a preheated oven to brown on all sides. You can also brown the meat in a frying pan, place in a roasting tin and put in a preheated oven. Evenly browned meat will be juicy. When roasting, baste it with marinade and cover with foil. Take out of the oven, wait a few minutes, cut into slices (with a sharp knife) and baste with the sauce from roasting in one of the following flavours: season the sauce from roasting with a tbsp of plum jam, add strained sauce left from the marinade, cook over a low heat until it thickens.

Make sauce from a handful of soaked dried mushrooms (cooked and sliced together with the stock) mixed with the sauces from roasting and the marinade. Cook until it thickens, and optionally add a few tbsp of thick cream and one tbsp of horseradish grated using a large-hole grater, scalded to remove the bitter taste.

In both options you need to season the dish with salt, a pinch of sugar and pepper.

Stew

Cut the meat into small pieces two hours prior, and add salt, allspice, thyme and pepper. Put aside. Stir-fry using half the melted butter, keeping in mind that butter burns easily and is then unusable. Brown flour in the remaining butter and mix with stock (or a vegetable stock cube dissolved in boiling water), heating until it thickens. Add the mustard, season to taste with salt and pepper, and combine with the cream. Now put the meat into the sauce and boil for 5 minutes. Serve at once. You can alter the flavour of the sauce slightly, replacing mustard with tomato concentrate, a pinch of sugar and a tbsp of lemon juice to taste. You can enrich it with olives, capers, finely chopped, blanched vegetables or onion. If you use a different kind of meat for the stew, it will have to be stewed longer to be tender, preferably in olive oil, and only then combined with the sauce and a tbsp of butter to give it a sophisticated flavour.

- 1 kg of beef (round steak or tenderloin)
- 50 ga of butter
- 2 glasses of vegetable stock
- 1 tbsp of flour
- 2 tbsp of cream
- 1 tbsp of mustard with seeds
- a pinch of allspice
- a pinch of thyme
- salt, pepper

Porterhouse steaks

600 g of tenderloin

½ glass of olive oil

1 tsp of Provençal herbs

salt, pepper

Mix the olive oil with the herbs and spread over the meat, then leave in the fridge for 24 hours. Heat a frying pan to a high temperature, cut the meat into 2-cm slices, knead lightly by hand (but be sure not to use a mallet) and fry on both sides in a frying pan. The question of how well done it should be depends on individual taste. Some people prefer their steak underdone inside and well done on the outside, while others like their meat fried long and well. Keep in mind that tenderloin fried over a low heat for a long time will be tougher and less juicy than when stir-fried over a high heat.

You can serve the steaks with fried onion or on a buttered slice of a bread roll, toasted in a frying pan or baked in the oven. The amount of salt and freshly ground pepper is also a question of individual taste. Tenderloin likes the company of freshly grated Parmesan cheese or forest fruit (cowberry, cranberry) and a slice of lemon. It tastes delicious with a wine-flavoured apple, sliced and cooked in butter with a pinch of fresh marjoram. You can also serve it with a slice of herb butter, made beforehand (you simply mix regular, soft butter with finely chopped herbs and shape it into a roll, wrap in aluminium foil and store in the fridge).

There are also fans of rubbing the frying pan used for making slices of toast with a clove of garlic cut in half, but in my opinion, you shouldn't obscure the flavour of such delicious meat.

Meatball with mushrooms

Soak a stale bread roll in vegetable stock (or a cube of vegetable stock dissolved in boiling water), press, and add to the minced meat. Soak the dried mushrooms in a small amount of water, cook in the same water, cut into small pieces, add to the meat and keep the stock for the sauce. Fry the onion in olive oil, season with salt and add to the meat. Mix the meat with a whole raw egg, parsley leaves, marjoram and pepper. Blend together, shape into a meatball and coat in breadcrumbs. You can simmer it or roast it. To simmer it, brown it on all sides in hot fat, baste with mushroom stock and cook covered over a low heat until tender. At the end thicken the sauce with cream mixed with flour. To roast the meatball, put it in a buttered mould, spread some fat on top, place in a hot oven and brown and then baste with the mushroom stock (save half a glass). Towards the end of roasting, mix cream with flour and half a glass of mushroom stock, baste the meatball and roast.

The best way to make a meatball is to use several types of meat. Instead of mushrooms you can add a tbsp of mustard with finely chopped raw pepper, and replace the mushroom stock with a vegetable one.

1 kg of minced meat

1 stale bread roll

1 glass of vegetable stock

1 egg

2-3 tbsp of breadcrumbs

2 tbsp of olive oil

a few dried mushrooms

½ glass of cream

1 tbsp of flour

1 tbsp of finely chopped parsl leaves

1 tsp of dried marjoram

salt, pepper

Cube steaks

1 kg of rump steak

½ glass of olive oil or some other cooking fat

a few dried mushrooms

1 onion

1 tbsp of tarragon

1 tbsp of horseradish

salt, pepper

For cube steaks you need a piece of tender beef, without veins and fat, so that the cutlets are juicy and tender. Cut 6-8 large slices crosswise to the muscle fibre (each one-centimetre thick). Pound slightly, give the right shape, add salt and pepper, coat with olive oil and put into a heated frying pan. Brown on both sides, but turn only once. Place the cutlets in a pot, cover with the stock from cooking the mushrooms soaked earlier, and add finely chopped mushrooms, onion and tarragon. Cook covered for an hour. In the meantime add peeled and scalded horseradish grated using a large-hole grater. Check on it regularly, turn the cutlets and make sure they have enough sauce, otherwise add a little water.

Fans of thick sauces should at the time add a roux made from butter and flour, or sprinkle the cutlets with flour before frying them.

Roast beef

1 kg of roast beef

½ glass of olive oil or a preferred kind

2 onions

salt, pepper

Coat the rinsed and boned meat with olive oil, cover with slices of onion and leave until the next day, remembering to turn it from time to time. Before roasting add a little salt and wrap the meat in aluminium foil before putting it in a preheated oven for about 2 hours. Prod the meat with a fork to see if it's tender. Sprinkle with white pepper before serving.

You can stud the meat with cloves of garlic cut in half, or with strips of pork fat (puncture the meat with the tip of a knife and place garlic or pork fat in the hole).

It tastes delicious with plum sauce as well. Melt a tbsp of butter in a saucepan, brown a tbsp of flour in it, mix with half a glass of cream and plums passed through a sieve. Season to taste with a glass of red wine, a pinch of sugar, salt and pepper, and mix with the sauce left from roasting the meat.

A few rosemary needles or another favourite herb added to the onion to marinate the meat will give it a unique flavour.

Beef collops

These are a flagship dish of Polish cuisine: pounded, rolled up, with all kinds of stuffing and sauces: onion, mushroom, tomato or gravyyour.

Slice the rinsed and dried meat, pound thoroughly into large pieces, sprinkle with lemon juice, spread with stuffing, roll up tightly, secure with cotton string, scald in boiling water, sprinkle with salt and pepper, and brown evenly in a frying pan with hot fat, preferably a tbsp of oil and a tbsp of butter. Oil has a higher burning temperature, but butter tastes great, so I use a mixture of both most of the time. Put into a saucepan, add the soup vegetables (without leek) grated using a large-hole grater, cover with a stock of soaked and boiled mushrooms and cook until tender – first covered and then without a lid, so that the sauce thickens. At the end add 2 tbsp of thick cream or a glass of dry wine to the strained sauce (thinned with boiling water if needed). Remove the string before serving.

Stuffing: soak a handful of dried mushrooms and cook them until tender in a small amount of water, just to cover them. When cooled down cut the mushrooms into small pieces and grind with finely chopped bacon. Mix with finely chopped onion fried in butter, add a tbsp of breadcrumbs, a raw egg, a tbsp of finely chopped parsley, and salt and pepper to taste.

You can replace the parsley with dried marjoram, and season the stuffing with a pinch of ground allspice.

Another way is to place the beef collops in the oven for about an hour and a half, covering them with foil so that they don't brown too much.

1 kg beef for collops
1 tbsp of lemon juice
3 tbsp of butter
1 tbsp of olive oil
1 egg
a few dried mushrooms
100 g of smoked bacon
1 tbsp of breadcrumbs
2 tbsp of cream or a glass of red wine
1 tbsp of parsley leaves
soup vegetables
salt, pepper

Beef roulades

1 kg culotte steak

½ l vegetable stock

2 tbsp of mustard

  a few pickled cucumbers

  a few slices of smoked bacon

2 tbsp of flour

  cooking oil

  salt, pepper

Slice the meat crosswise to the fibre, pound, add salt, rub with mustard on one side and top with a thin slice of smoked bacon and a piece of a cucumber cut in strips. Roll up tightly, secure with a pin or wrap using string. Coat in flour and stir-fry in hot fat. When the meat browns place in a taller pot, pour in stock and the cooking sauce and then stew over a low heat for an hour and a half. Turn a couple of times when stewing and add hot water if the sauce evaporates.

You can also wrap the roulades with dried plum (soaked earlier), onion and a strip of pork fat. You can add variety to the sauce with a few tbsp of cream, or make the roulades in tomato sauce.

Beef roulades 2

Cut the rinsed and dried meat crosswise to the fibres, pound into thin slices, sprinkle with salt and pepper, and set aside while you prepare the stuffing. Take the white raw sausage out of its casing, mix in a bowl with the horseradish, grated wholemeal bread and cream, which can be replaced with a tbsp of oil. Season with a pinch of salt and pepper. Place a roll of stuffing on top of the meat cut and roll up tightly, securing with string. Heat fat in a saucepan to a high temperature, coat roulades in flour and fry, turning evenly, add onion cut in cubes, vegetable stock (or a vegetable stock cube dissolved in water) and cook covered over a low heat for an hour and a half. Towards the end season the sauce with ketchup, mixed with cream and cook together for a while longer.

If white sausage is not aromatic enough, you can add half a tsp of marjoram or a clove of garlic strained through a garlic press to the stuffing.

1 kg culotte steak
2 tbsp of flour
1 onion
15 g of white sausage
2 tbsp of horseradish
1 tbsp grated wholemeal bread
2 tbsp of cream
2 tbsp of ketchup
4 tbsp of olive oil for frying
½ l vegetable stock
salt, pepper

Beef shin

Steep sliced mushrooms in boiling water, cover the pot and leave for a couple of minutes. If you're using whole dried mushroom caps, you have to soak them for a couple of hours and cook until tender. Divide meat into small pieces (to shorten the cooking time), rub with salt, pepper, herbs and garlic strained through a garlic press. Brown on all sides on heated fat, add onions cut into quarters, pour in the stock with mushrooms and cook covered over a low heat for about 2 hours. It's only then that it will become glutinous and very tender. Add water to the sauce during cooking.

You can enrich the sauce by adding a glass of mead.

1½ kg of beef shin
1 bag of sliced dried mushrooms (20 g)
1 tbsp of herbs (marjoram, oregano, Provençal herbs)
1 clove of garlic
2 onions
2 tbsp of cooking fat
salt, pepper

Stuffed calf's brisket

1 calf's brisket

3 tbsp of breadcrumbs

3 tbsp of butter

1 egg

1 tsp of marjoram

3 tbsp of finely chopped parsley
or dill

salt, pepper

To make the stuffing, blend two tbsp of butter and mix with breadcrumbs, an egg, parsley or dill. Rinse and drain off the meat, and rub with marjoram and salt. Separate a cut of meat from the ribs (making a small cut with a sharp knife) and place the stuffing in the pocket created. Put into a preheated oven spread with the rest of the butter. You can surround it with potatoes and bake them with the meat. Add butter and water several times during roasting. You can also make the stuffing from raisins and plums soaked earlier, mixed with a bread roll, soaked in milk and pressed.

Another recipe for the stuffing is to make it from minced meat seasoned with herbs, fried onion, breadcrumbs and a yolk with egg whites whipped to a froth.

Also slightly blanched Brussels sprouts, sprinkled with powdered garlic can make a stuffing.

Stuffed veal

Cut the rinsed and dried meat lengthwise, and rub with marjoram, salt and pepper. Set aside while you prepare the stuffing. Blend cottage cheese with a yolk, breadcrumbs, finely chopped figs and thyme. Season with salt and pepper, finishing with egg whites whipped to a froth. Put the stuffing on the meat cut, cover it with another one and secure it with string. Place the meat in a roasting tin, spread butter over it and put into a preheated oven. When the roast is browned, reduce the heat, pour in some vegetable stock (or a vegetable stock cube dissolved in boiling water) and roast for 2 hours. Remove the string before serving.

1 kg of meat for a roast

50 g of cottage cheese

1 tsp of thyme

a few dried figs

1 tbsp of breadcrumbs

1 egg

1 tsp of marjoram

½ glass of vegetable stock

2 tbsp of butter

salt, pepper

Stewed veal

1 kg meat (preferably loin of veal or forequarter, as it will be more glutinous than rump)

2 cloves of garlic

½ tsp of marjoram

salt, pepper

2 tbsp of butter

2 tbsp of olive oil

Rub the rinsed and dried meat with salt, pepper, marjoram and a clove of garlic strained through a garlic press. Brown it evenly on all sides in hot fat. Pour a glass of hot water and stew, covered, for about 2 hours, turning the meat and adding water regularly. The veal will be really delicious if you add a glass of dry white wine to the sauce towards the end.

Stewed veal shank

Take the rinsed and drained veal shanks (cleaned of any tiny chips of bones, which are often left after chopping), rub the meat with herbs and pepper, and stir-fry in heated fat on all sides. If you don't have time to brown the onion and garlic separately, you can put it into a frying pan with the meat and brown for a while over a reduced heat and then add vegetable stock (or a vegetable stock cube dissolved in boiling water) and wine. Mix together, season to taste with salt, keeping in mind that the stock is salty, cover with a lid and stew over low heat for over an hour, until the meat becomes glutinous and very tender. This veal can be seasoned with a tbsp of cream to give it a delicate flavour, and sprinkled with finely chopped parsley before serving.

Another version of this recipe is to serve the meat with tomato sauce, i.e. adding a few peeled tomatoes (fresh or canned) towards the end of cooking. In my opinion the veal tastes best with 2 tbsp of garlic sauce with honey. You should add it during cooking, when the meat is already tender. This slightly sweet, thick sauce brings out the delicious flavour of veal shank.

4 small veal shanks

3 tbsp of cooking fat

2 cloves of garlic

1 onion

1 tsp of marjoram

1 tsp of oregano

1 glass of vegetable stock

½ glass of dry white wine

salt, pepper

Liver with apples

600 g of liver

½ glass of flour

2 tbsp of butter

2 tbsp of olive oil

2 cooking apples

1 glass of mead

a handful of raisins

1 tbsp of butter

1 tsp of fresh marjoram leaves or a pinch of dried marjoram

salt, pepper

Cut the washed and peeled apples into small pieces and cook in a saucepan with a tbsp of butter, 2 tbsp of water and a glass of mead, until the apples are half done and the sauce thickens. Set aside for a while. Cut the meat (rinsed, drained, and with any membranes removed) into slices. Melt the fat in a frying pan, coat the cuts of meat in flour and fry on both sides according to taste, although they shouldn't be too well done. When the cuts are ready add salt and freshly ground pepper. Lay out on a serving dish, surround with the apples stewed in butter and raisins, stir-fried in the frying pan in which you fried the liver. Raisins stir-fried in butter are not a necessary side dish, but they perfectly bring out the flavour of this delicate meat, and so will a garnish of a few fresh marjoram leaves.

Fans of classic flavour combinations serve liver with stewed or browned onion.

Pork in mustard sauce

1 kg of pork ham

1 clove of garlic

1 onion

1 glass of vegetable stock

a pinch of ground allspice

4 pickled gherkins

salt, pepper

3 tbsp of cooking fat

salt, pepper

1 tsp of white vinegar

1 tsp of mustard

200 ml of cream

Add a pinch of salt to the rinsed and drained meat, brown in a saucepan in heated fat with a sliced clove of garlic. Add finely chopped onion, which will overcook during cooking. After a while pour in vegetable stock (or a vegetable stock cube dissolved in boiling water) and cook over a low heat for more than an hour, until the meat becomes tender. Mix the cream with the mustard, pour into the sauce, add gherkins, cut into small pieces, season with salt, pepper and vinegar and cook without a lid for a few minutes so that the sauce thickens. This pork tastes best with potatoes baked in herbs.

Pork with plums

Brown the (rinsed and drained) meat on all sides in hot fat. Pour in water, vinegar and wine, add all the spices as well as plums and cook covered over a low heat, until the meat is tender.

Take the plums out and if not overcooked, strain through a sieve, add breadcrumbs browned in butter, thin with the roasting juices, and season with cinnamon. Cut the roast into slices when done and pour hot sauce over them on a serving dish. You can improve the sauce with a tbsp of plum jam.

1½ kg of pork ham
½ glass of dry white wine
½ glass of wine vinegar
1 glass of water
3 bay leaves
a few seeds of allspice
a few juniper berries
a handful of dried plums
1 tbsp of breadcrumbs
1 tbsp of butter
1 tbsp of olive oil
1 tsp of sugar
a pinch of cinnamon
salt

Pork loin chops coated with breadcrumbs

1 pork loin

2 eggs

2 tbsp of milk

1 glass of breadcrumbs

½ tsp of garlic powder

2 tbsp of cooking olive oil

2 tbsp of butter

salt, pepper

Rinse the meat and drain it off, removing fat and veins, then cut into 1.5-cm thick chops and pound by hand.

Break the eggs, mix them with milk and salt in one plate and pour breadcrumbs onto the other. Melt the butter with olive oil in a frying pan. Put the chops in the hot fat, first coating them in egg, then in breadcrumbs and then in egg again. After a few minutes, when they begin to brown, turn over and sprinkle with the dried garlic, salt and pepper. Serve warm, but they taste just as good cold.

Pork loin is delicious meat when marinated with herbs and rubbed with olive oil and it requires short roasting. Chops grilled in a grill pan are ready after a few minutes.

Pork knuckle cooked in beer

Rinse and clean the pork knuckles thoroughly and put them into boiling beer with water, clove and a bay leaf. After one hour of cooking, add peeled soup vegetables or a vegetable stock cube and a sliced clove of garlic and cook until the meat is tender, i.e. for at least another hour. Season the sauce left from cooking to taste with the caramel, salt and pepper, remove the lid and cook the meat until the sauce thickens.

You can also cook pork knuckles in broth before rubbing them with marjoram and garlic and roasting in the oven, while basting them with dark beer to create a crunchy skin on the surface of the meat. Another way is to brown the pork knuckles in heated fat, place them in the oven and pour water over them for the first hour, followed by beer for the second.

4 small pork knuckles
  soup vegetables
1 bottle of light beer
1 glass of water
1 bay leaf
1 clove of garlic
1 clove
1 teaspoon of caramel
  salt, pepper

Pork loin with mushrooms

Soak the dried mushrooms in a small amount of hot water and leave overnight (larger ones) or for one hour (if cut into thin slices) and then cook. Cut large ones into small pieces and leave in the stock. Rinse the pork loins, remove fat, drain, cut into a centimetre-thick slices, pound, and mix thoroughly with olive oil and pepper. Fry in a hot frying pan 2 minutes on each side so that the pork loins stay very tender and slightly pink inside. Put them into a bowl and add butter to the frying pan. Fry the finely chopped and salted onion. When golden, add the cooked mushrooms with the stock, mix together, pour in a glass of mead and cook for a while over a low heat so that the sauce becomes thicker. Blend with thick cream, and season to taste with salt and pepper. Put the pork loins in the sauce, warm up the whole dish and serve.

1 large or 2 small pork
  loin cuts
2 tbsp of oil
2 tbsp of butter
1 onion
20 g of dried mushrooms
1 glass of mead
200 ml of thick cream
  salt, pepper

- 200 g of minced pork
- 200 g of minced poultry
- 200 g of beef
- 1 large or 2 smaller onions
- 2 tbsp of butter
- 1 egg
- salt, pepper
- a pinch of your favourite herb, e.g. marjoram
- 1 stale bread roll
- ½ glass of milk or stock
- ½ glass of breadcrumbs
- 4 tbsp of cooking fat

Meat patties

The most delicious meat patties are made using three kinds of minced meat

Soak the bread roll in milk or stock. Fry the finely chopped and salted onion in butter. In a bowl mix the various kinds of minced meat with a raw egg, the pressed roll and onion, together with the butter from frying. Add spices to taste and knead into a smooth pulp. Form oblong patties of the same size using hands rinsed in cold water. Heat the cooking fat in a frying pan, coat the patties thoroughly in breadcrumbs, flatten slightly and give a chequered pattern with a knife, and put in the frying pan. Fry for a couple of minutes in very hot fat until brown, turn, and at the end put the lid on so that they are well done and juicy.

You can add variety to this recipe by putting finely chopped bell pepper cooked with onion, mushrooms and pickled cucumbers inside the patties.

Roasted ribs

Cook the ribs until tender in stock with a bay leaf, allspice and pepper. Take out and place in a heat-resistant dish, pour in the sauce and roast in the oven. The sauce is made with a glass of the stock from roasting the ribs, mixed with tomato concentrate, honey, lemon juice, basil, and salt and pepper to taste. You can add variety to the sauce with one finely chopped celery stalk and a clove of garlic.

You can also grill the cooked ribs, but before putting them on a rack you need to rub them with the sauce made by mixing spicy ketchup and honey.

Another recipe for a great dish is to cook the ribs in a stoneware roasting tin (thoroughly soaked in water beforehand). Just put layers of raw potatoes, onion, ribs and herbs in it. The dish has to be roasted for a long time at a low temperature.

1 kg of ribs

1 l vegetable stock

1 bay leaf

a few seeds of allspice

a few peppercorns

2 tbsp of tomato concentrate

1 tbsp of honey

½ tsp of dried basil

1 tbsp of lemon juice

salt, pepper

Stuffed cabbage in tomato sauce

½ kg of minced meat

a decent-sized head of savoy or white cabbage

1 tbsp of breadcrumbs

1 tsp of oregano

chives

3 tbsp of spicy ketchup

2 tbsp of olive oil

½ kg fresh tomatoes of whole canned tomatoes

1 glass of vegetable stock

½ tsp of basil

1 clove of garlic

a pinch of chilli pepper

1 tbsp of honey

1 tbsp of lemon juice

salt, pepper

Put the washed head of cabbage (without the cabbage stalk) into a large pot of boiling water, scald and leave to cool a little. In this way you will be able to remove the outer leaves and keep them crisp.

Again scald and remove the outer leaves. You can also heat the cabbage in a large saucepan over a low heat and remove the leaves one by one. Cut out the nerve connected to the cabbage stalk carefully so that you don't make holes in the leaves. Prepare the stuffing by adding to the mincemeat: oregano, breadcrumbs, finely chopped chives, 2 tbsp of spicy ketchup, salt and pepper to taste.

Knead to a pulp and put it on the cabbage leaves, then fold in the sides and roll up like croquettes. You can add variety to the stuffing with finely chopped bell pepper or rice cooked earlier. Another delicious kind of stuffing is one with onion with herbs cooked in clarified butter.

Heat oil in a pot, add a sliced clove of garlic, cover the bottom with a few cabbage leaves (to prevent it from burning) and put the stuffed cabbage inside, packing tightly. Pour tomato sauce over it, i.e. a glass of vegetable stock with tomato concentrate, basil, chilli, spicy ketchup, honey and lemon juice. Top it with canned or peeled tomatoes, or fresh tomatoes cut into small pieces. Cover the pot with a lid and cook over a low heat for about 45 minutes. Use the rest of the cabbage head for other dishes, or cut into quarters and add to the stewed stuffed cabbage.

You can also make the same dish using savoy cabbage in mushroom sauce or your own sauce, e.g. cooked with a glass of vegetable stock and half a glass of white wine, season to taste with salt, pepper and thyme.

Another recipe for a filling is cooked buckwheat groats mixed with fried onion with herbs.

Loin of pork with apples

1 kg of loin pork

1 tsp of marjoram

3 tbsp of cooking fat

3 apples (Reinette apple is the best choice)

1 glass of vegetable stock

salt, pepper

Rub the (rinsed and drained) loin of pork with salt, pepper and marjoram, keeping in mind that if you cover the meat with vegetable stock from a cube, you don't need much salt as the stock is already salty. Another way is to rub the loin of pork with a clove of garlic strained through a sieve. Brown it evenly on all sides in hot fat and then pour in the vegetable stock, and add the apples (washed, peeled, and cut into small pieces and with cores removed). Cook covered over a low heat until the meat is tender.

Tongue in horseradish sauce

You can use beef or the more delicate pork tongue, but veal tongue is the best choice. Rinse the meat thoroughly, scald with boiling water and cook until tender with soup vegetables, a bay leaf, allspice, salt and pepper. When the meat cools, skin it (if the meat is tender, the skin comes off easily) and cut into slices. You can put them into a heat-resistant dish, steeped in the stock from cooking., Garnish with carrot and place in a preheated oven for 15 minutes, or lay out on a dish and pour congealing jelly over it, made from the cooking stock strained through a sieve, and leave in the fridge for the jelly to set. A good idea is to serve the tongue cut into slices with horseradish sauce.

Horseradish sauce: make a roux from two tbsp of butter and one tbsp of flour, i.e. brown the flour in melted fat, add a glass of stock from cooking, 4 tbsp of freshly grated horseradish, a tbsp of lemon juice and a tsp of sugar, and keep over a low heat for a couple of minutes until it thickens. Turn off the heat and add half a glass of cream mixed with a raw yolk. Blend well and pour over the meat. The same sauce can also be used with beef cooked in broth.

1 kg of tongue

soup vegetables

a bay leaf

a few seeds of allspice

2 tbsp of butter

1 tsp of flour

4 tbsp of horseradish

1 tbsp of lemon juice

200 ml of cream

1 yolk

salt, pepper, sugar

White sausage in wine

White sausage has a long tradition in Poland, particularly as it is served during the Easter breakfast. Originally it was eaten boiled or roasted with finely chopped onion.

Fry the whole white sausage in oil, cover with red wine, add rosemary and honey and cook over a low heat without the lid until the wine evaporates, the sauce thickens and the sausages are brown. Add the olives and cook for a few minutes together. Serve garnished with a sprig of rosemary.

1 kg of white sausage

1 bottle of dry red wine

3 tbsp of olive oil

1 tbsp of black olives

1 tbsp of finely chopped rosemary

1 tbsp of honey

Chicken thighs in cream

4 chicken thighs or 8 drumsticks

2 tbsp of cooking butter

a few shallots

1 carton of double cream

1 tsp of flour

1 tbsp of butter

1 yolk

1 tbsp of finely chopped parsley leaves

½ lemon

¾ glass of vegetable stock

salt, white pepper

Rub the rinsed and dried thighs with juice from half a lemon and salt. Melt the butter in a saucepan and brown the thighs, add the peeled, whole shallots, and after a short while pour in the stock (or a stock cube dissolved in boiling water). Cook covered over a low heat until the meat is tender. Mix the cream with the flour and a raw yolk, pour over the thighs, mix and cook together for a while. Before serving season to taste with salt and white pepper. Garnish on a serving dish with parsley leaves and lemon peel cut into thin strips or grated using a zester.

De volaille

Take the rinsed and dried breasts and carefully cut lengthwise. Pound with a mallet. Put a piece of blue cheese in the centre of each, together with some frozen butter. Roll up tightly, pressing the edges in, so that the butter does not melt out during frying. Heat the oil in a frying pan, coat the breasts in flour and eggs whisked with a pinch of salt and breadcrumbs. Fry in very hot oil until golden, turning evenly. Sprinkle with freshly ground pepper before serving.

You can stuff chicken breast cutlets with all kinds of ingredients, e.g. a slice of ham or Swiss cheese. Another way is to spread a little mustard, ketchup or honey inside the breasts and serve them with a slice of lemon or sauces.

400 g of chicken breast

2 tbsp of flour

2 eggs

3 tbsp of breadcrumbs

1 tbsp of blue cheese

1 tbsp of butter

4 tbsp of cooking olive oil

salt, pepper

Roast chicken

1 chicken

¼ glass of flour

1 egg

2 tbsp of breadcrumbs

100 ga of butter

Stuffing:

2 tbsp of butter

2 eggs

1 tbsp of finely chopped parsley

1 tbsp of finely chopped dill

5 tbsp of breadcrumbs

salt, pepper

Take a rinsed and dried chicken, rub it with pepper and stuff with a mixture of raw eggs blended with butter, breadcrumbs, parsley leaves, dill. Season with salt and pepper. Whisk the egg whites and add at the end to make the stuffing more fluffy. When the chicken is stuffed and sewn up, sprinkle it with flour and pour a raw egg over it, ending with breadcrumbs. Place in a roasting tin with butter and put into a preheated oven. Roast, frequently basting with fresh butter.

Don't pour water or stock over the chicken as it won't be crispy then.

You can add finely chopped onion, fried in butter, as well as poultry liver.

To speed up the process cut a rinsed and dried chicken in half, firmly press, rub with salt, pepper and a drop of oil, place in a heat-resistant dish skin up, and sprinkle with herbs (thyme, rosemary, sage). Put segments of lemon around it with slightly crushed cloves of garlic, place in an oven preheated to 200 degrees Celsius and roast for 40 minutes (if the skin gets dark brown, cover with a piece of foil).

Marinated duck

1 duck

3 tbsp of clarified butter

salt

Marinade:

½ glass of red wine

a few peppercorns

a few seeds of allspice

1 tbsp of lemon juice

1 tsp of finely cut ginger root

2 cloves

1 bay leaf

1 onion

1 clove of garlic

1 carrot

1 parsley

a piece of celeriac

Boil a glass of water in a saucepan and add vegetables grated using a large grater: carrot, parsley, celeriac and sliced onion. During cooking (about half an hour in total) successively add the ginger, garlic and the rest of the spices, ending with the wine and lemon juice or wine vinegar. Cool and rub the rinsed and dried duck with it thoroughly. Leave in the fridge for two days (or at least a few hours), turning it regularly on both sides so that the marinade is absorbed evenly by the meat, making it aromatic and tender.

Take the duck out of the marinade, dry off slightly, rub with salt (leave it in salt for half an hour at room temperature) and cover with butter. Place in a preheated oven, brown, reduce heat and roast for about two hours. You can pour roasting sauce or marinade over it. The sauce for the marinated duck can be made using a traditional recipe by preparing a roux from one tbsp of caramel and one tbsp of flour with the roasting juices, the marinade, half a glass of vegetable stock, and finally adding two tbsp of sour cream.

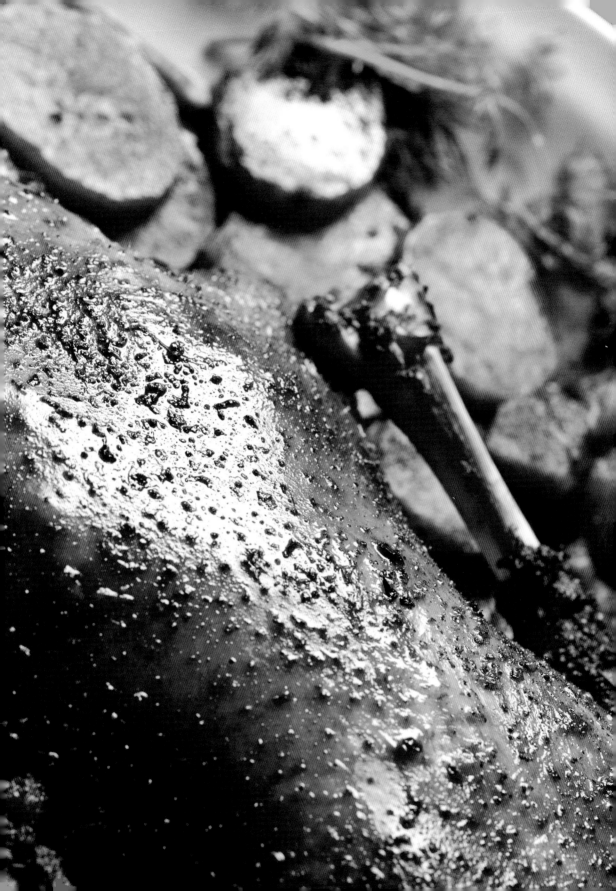

Duck with apples

Take a rinsed, dried and thoroughly plucked duck and thoroughly rub it inside and out with a mixture of marjoram, pepper, salt, cumin, allspice and olive oil (preferably a few hours before roasting). Put the washed apples inside (cut into quarters with the skin, but without cores) and then sew up or secure with a skewer. You can spread some fat over the duck and put into a preheated oven, but it will be much more tasty if you put it on a spit, tying the duck using string, so that the wings or legs don't fall down. A duck secured at both ends in this manner will turn around smoothly, its skin will become crispy, and it will lose much more fat. You can serve it with cranberry or cowberry jam, or a side dish of apples briefly cooked in butter.

1 duck

1 tbsp of marjoram

   a pinch of ground cumin

   a pinch of allspice

2 large cooking apples

2 tbsp of olive oil

   salt, pepper

Marinated duck breasts with skin

4 duck breasts with skin

2 tbsp of olive oil

a few red pepper cornsseeds

1 bay leaf

1 tbsp of marjoram

Rinse and dry the breasts thoroughly. Rub them with a mixture of olive oil, marjoram, a crumbled bay leaf and red pepper. Leave in the fridge for 24 hours or at least a couple of hours. Cut the skin in several places using a sharp knife and put the breasts skin down in a very hot frying pan. After a few minutes, when they get dark brown, turn and fry on the other side. The rest of the recipe depends on individual taste. You make cuts in the breasts so that they keep their original shape, and pour sauce over them. Meat cooked in this way is tender, but slightly underdone inside. Another way is to cook them in a frying pan for about 20 minutes more, first pouring a glass of vegetable stock over them (or a vegetable stock cube dissolved in boiling water), a glass of dry red wine, a tsp of honey and a tbsp of lemon juice. You can garnish the dish with thin strips of orange peel and serve with cranberry, orange or raspberry sauce.

Roasted hare in cream sauce

Rub the cleaned hare with a marinade from soup vegetables grated on a large-hole grater, sliced onion, pepper, juniper, allspice and a bay leaf. Set aside in a cool place for a couple of hours. If it wasn't soaked in buttermilk, you can add a tbsp of lemon juice to the marinade and keep the hare in it longer, remembering to turn it over so that the marinade ingredients cover the meat evenly. Take out, remove vegetables, add salt, cover with butter in a roasting tin or a heat-resistant dish with a lid and put into a preheated oven. During roasting baste the meat with the juices collecting at the bottom of the dish. When the meat is tender, divide it into pieces, put into a saucepan and cover with the sauce made by mixing the roasting juices and cream, blended with a tbsp of flour (flour is not necessary). Meat prepared in this way has to be cooked under a lid with the sauce. If the sauce is too thick, you can thin it, or add variety to it by pouring in half a glass of mushroom stock.

1 gamey hare, i.e. stored for a few days at a low temperature, preferably somewhere well ventilated. After skinning and gutting it the hare should be left in buttermilk for two days.

a few crushed juniper berries

a few seeds of allspice

1 bay leaf

1 onion

1 carrot

1 parsley

a piece of celeriac

100 g of butter

200 ml of sour cream

1 tsp of flour

salt, pepper

Turkey hen with a classic stuffing

1 frozen turkey hen

2 tbsp of lemon juice

100 g of stale bread roll

1 glass of milk

turkey liver

about 500 g of chicken livers

3 eggs

2 tbsp of butter

2 tbsp of chopped parsley leaves or dill

1 tbsp of icing sugar

a pinch of nutmeg

1 tsp of marjoram

salt, pepper

Thaw a turkey hen overnight, rinse, dry and rub with lemon juice, marjoram, salt and pepper. Leave for two hours. Press the roll soaked in milk, and mince it with the turkey and chicken livers. Blend the butter with three yolks, add the liver with the roll, parsley leaves, sugar, salt, pepper, nutmeg to taste and egg whites whipped to a froth. If the stuffing is too thin, you can add a tbsp of breadcrumbs. Stuff the turkey hen and sew it up. Roast covered for more than two hours, basting it with melted sauce. If it gets brown too quickly, pour water or wine over it. If it takes too long, take the lid off.

The stuffing for the turkey hen can also include a handful of almonds (scalded, with the skin removed) and a handful of raisins, rinsed and scalded earlier. Depending on your culinary tastes, you can also add one ground clove or a few juniper berriesseeds.

In the old days, stuffing from Cracow groats was very popular: blend a raw egg and a glass of Cracow groats, pour in half a litre of vegetable stock and boil. Cut 10 g of pork fat into small pieces and melt the scratchings. Mix with groats, add a tbsp of chopped dill and bake in the oven for half an hour. Add a tbsp of marjoram and finely chopped liver to this aromatic groats dish, mix together and season.

Turkey hen with roasted meat stuffing

1 turkey hen

1 onion

2 tbsp of butter

100 g of pork fat

4 anchovy fillets

1 bread roll

½ glass of milk

200 g of roasted veal

2 eggs

1 tbsp of capers

1 tbsp of lemon juice

1 tsp of marjoram

a pinch of ground nutmeg

2 tbsp of cooking fat (butter or oil)

salt, pepper

Soak the stale roll in milk. Rub the turkey hen (rinsed and dried) inside and out with salt and marjoram. Sprinkle it with lemon juice and set aside while you prepare the stuffing. Cook the finely chopped and salted onion in butter. Mince the meat cut into pieces with pork fat, cooked onion, together with the butter from cooking, the pressed roll and the fillets. Add whole eggs, salt, pepper, a pinch of nutmeg and whole capers and blend the stuffing together well. Stuff the turkey hen with it, sew it up or fasten with a skewer. Rub with olive oil or pour melted butter over it and place in a roasting tin. Put in a preheated oven for over two hours, first to brown the meat and then reducing the heat and basting it regularly.

The stuffing will have a slightly different flavour if you skip the anchovies and cook onion with smoked bacon, cut into small pieces.

1 bottle of dry red wine

1 glass of water

1 glass of sugar

½ a vanilla pod

a few cloves

12 dried figs

10 dried plums

a handful of raisins

4 pears

Christmas Eve compote with wine

Boil the red wine with the sugar, water, cloves and a vanilla pod cut in half, add figs and boil over a low heat for 10 minutes, add plums and boil for a few minutes more. Add raisins at the end. This is a recipe for a delicious compote, which can be prepared a few hours in advance, but if you have more time, you can improve it by adding a few pears and blanching them for a few minutes, making sure, however, they are not overcooked. You can serve the fruit separately, garnished with whipped cream or in a compote. You can also decorate it with lemon or orange peel cut into thin strips. For a traditional compote, when covering the fruit with water, add a glass of fruit syrup and a tbsp of thin strips of lemon or orange peel (without the white pulp).

Pears in chocolate

Boil water with the sugar, a few cloves and a pinch of cinnamon. Add the washed, peeled pears without cores and cut in half. Boil for a few minutes over a low heat, so that a fork goes in easily but they are not too soft. Take them out with a strainer and set aside for a few minutes to cool slightly. Put a tsp of jam into the core hole. Place on a serving dish or in dessert bowls, flat side down. Sprinkle with lemon juice and pour chocolate sauce over the fruit. In a small saucepan melt the sugar and vanilla sugar, mix with 3 tbsp of pear compote, add mead and cocoa and heat, stirring constantly to make a thick, smooth sauce. The sauce will be more unique if at the end you add "kogel mogel" from two yolks (a confection made of raw egg yolk and sugar). Garnish with almond flakes browned in a dry frying pan, and raisins. Set aside to cool completely.

4 large pears

a pinch of cinnamon

a few cloves

1 heaped tbsp of sugar

2 tbsp of lemon juice

8 tsp of jam

50 ga of butter

2 tbsp of sugar

2 tbsp of cocoa

1 packet of vanilla sugar

1 glass of mead

a handful of raisins

a handful of almond flakes

Dough:

2 glasses of flour

4 tbsp of icing sugar

100 g of butter

1 egg

1 yolk

1 tbsp of lemon zest

Chocolate coating glaze:

2 tbsp of sugar

3 tbsp of cocoa

1 tsp of butter

¼ glass of milk

Short-crust tarts

Dough: chop the butter with flour and sugar to get a "sandy" consistency, add a yolk, a whole egg and zest from a scalded lemon. Knead the dough quickly, wrap in foil and leave in the fridge for at least one hour (you can make it a day or even two days earlier).

Take it out from the fridge, roll out into ½ cm thick layers (preferably between two pieces of transparent foil). Cut out round cookies with a glass. Make holes in half of them with a shot glass. Bake all the cookies in an oven heated to a medium temperature (170-180°C) until light golden.

Coating glaze: sprinkle the sugar with the milk and melt over heat, stirring constantly. Blend the cocoa with cold milk, add to the melted sugar and stir over heat until smooth and quite thick. Remove from the heat, add butter and stir.

Sprinkle the baked cookies that have holes with icing sugar. Spread coating glaze over the rest and put the cookies with holes on top.

You can replace the coating glaze with good-quality thick jam.

Yeast cake

Beat the yolks over steam with sugar until white. Mix half a glass of flour with a tsp of sugar and yeast ground down in milk. Make leaven with the consistency of double cream and set aside in a warm place for half an hour. Add the flour, vanilla and salt to whisked eggs; mix, blend with the leaven and knead the dough thoroughly. Cover with a cloth and leave in a warm place to rise. When it does, pour in clarified butter, add rinsed and scalded raisins, knead for about 15 minutes and again leave to rise. When it doubles in volume smear two smaller or one large mould with fat, put the dough in, and when it rises again place it in a preheated oven and bake for about an hour at 180°C.

6 yolks

¼ milk of glass

60 g of yeast

250 g of flour

200 g of sugar

100 g of butter

½ vanilla pod

50 g of raisins

a pinch of salt

Michalina's cake

¼ kg of flour

40 g of yeast

1 glass of milk

100 g of butter

100 g of sugar

100 g of almonds

½ vanilla pod

3 eggs

breadcrumbs to sprinkle over the mould

1 tbsp of butter to spread over the mould

Mix the ground yeast thoroughly with warm milk and two tbsp of flour and leave in a warm place. Beat the yolks with sugar over steam until white. The best way is to put a bowl with yolks into a sieve, placed in a large pot filled with boiling water. When the leaven rises, add the whisked yolks, chopped almonds (without skin or almond flakes) and vanilla; knead the dough. Add the warm clarified butter and knead the dough for another 30 minutes. At the end add the egg whites whisked to a stiff froth and delicately mix with the dough. Place in a buttered mould, sprinkle with breadcrumbs and leave in a warm place to rise. Put in a preheated oven and bake for about an hour.

After it cools down you can ice it. To make the icing, mix the icing sugar with water and warm up, stirring constantly. When it begins to thicken, add: (at one's own discretion) lemon juice, almond oil, cocoa and orange liqueur. Before it sets you can garnish the cake with almond flakes, candied lemon peel or raisins.

Apple cookies

Chop sifted flour with butter for a "sandy" consistency. Add blended cottage cheese, knead dough thoroughly, roll up, cut into squares, place a piece of an apple in the centre of each square (washed, peeled and without a core). Press the corners together to make little rectangular pillows. Leave one smaller side open, with the apple slightly sticking out to let off steam. Put on a greased baking tin, place in a preheated oven and bake until golden. Take out and sprinkle with icing sugar.

½ kg flour

½ kg butter

½ kg low-fat cottage cheese

4 apples

a pinch of salt

icing sugar

An easy recipe for a chocolate Easter cake

- 1 bag of chocolate short-crust pastry tarts
- 100 g of butter
- 3 bars of plain chocolate
- 4 tbsp of water
- 4 tbsp of cognac or another kind of alcohol
- a large carton of mascarpone cheese (50 g)

Melt the butter in a saucepan and add the crumbled tarts. Blend well and spread in a thin layer over a cake tin. Pour water into another saucepan, add the crumbled bars of chocolate and keep for a short while over a low heat so that the chocolate melts. Mix with the alcohol, remove from the heat and mix with the mascarpone cheese. Spread chocolate glazing on the bottom. Wrap a cake tin in foil and leave in the fridge for 3 hours to let it congeal. You can decorate this Easter cake with almond flakes browned in a dry frying pan, or cherries from a preserve, but it is just as delicious without.

Dulce de leche Easter cake

Chop the sifted flour with the butter and sugar, add the yolks and cream and quickly knead and shape the dough into a ball. Leave in the fridge for at least half an hour. Roll up, shaping into a rectangle. Put on a greased, flat baking tin and shape the edges. You can also put it into a cake tin, folding the edges. Place in an oven preheated to 200°C. Bake until golden.

Boil the milk and butter in a saucepan over a low heat until it thickens, then add butter and stir. Pour onto the cooled dough. Optionally, garnish with walnut halves.

- 350 g flour
- ½ glass of sugar
- 200 g of butter or margarine
- 1 tbsp of sour cream
- 2 yolks
- 1 pinch of salt

Coating:

- 2 glasses of milk
- 100 g of butter
- 2 glasses of sugar

400 ml can of peaches

½ kg of whole-milk or semi-
-skimmed cottage cheese

3 eggs

5 g of raisins

1 ½ glasses of icing sugar

2 tbsp of butter

1 packet of fruit jelly

300 g of sponge fingers

Cold peach cheesecake

Prepare the jelly following the instructions on the packet. Blend the butter with the icing sugar and yolks, add minced cottage cheese and blend until smooth. Add half of the cool but still liquid jelly to the cheese, as well as the egg whites whipped into a froth and stir. Leave 1-2 peaches for decoration, cut the rest into pieces and add to the cheese. Mix together.

Cover a small cake tin with the sponge fingers. Put the cheese in the cake tin, and top with peaches and raisins. Pour the setting jelly over it. Leave in the fridge for 3-4 hours.

My sister's cheesecake

Blend the cheese with the butter, add dry custard and baking powder. Mix the yolks with sugar and blend with the cheese. Whip the egg whites into a stiff froth and add to the dough. Rinse and drain the raisins, mix them with the potato flour and add to the cheese. Mix all the ingredients together, and put into a buttered cake tin sprinkled with breadcrumbs. Put in a slightly heated oven and bake for an hour at 180°C. Open the oven door slightly and slowly cool the cake so it doesn't sink.

1 kg semi-skimmed cottage cheese

200 g of butter

8 yolks

1½ glasses of sugar

¾ tsp of baking powder

1 custard

6 egg whites

100 g of raisins

fat and breadcrumbs for the mould

Pascha

(a sweet Easter dish made of cottage cheese and dried fruit)

1 kg of cottage cheese

5 yolks

300 g of icing sugar

250 ml cream

200 g of butter

100 g of almond flakes

100 g of raisins

½ vanilla pod

lemon juice

1 shot glass of vodka – 25 ml

candied fruit

Mince or blend the cottage cheese (whole-milk, non-sour, well-pressed). Blend five yolks with the icing sugar, add cream, heat (while stirring, preferably over steam, but not bringing them to the boil) until it thickens, remove from the heat, and blend with the butter (defrosted and soft). Add the cottage cheese, almond flakes, raisins rinsed in boiling water, a finely chopped vanilla pod, lemon juice, a shot glass of vodka (or strong rum). Blend together well; line a sieve with a linen cloth, put the dough in it and press (with a cutting board or a small plate loaded down with a jar filled with water), leave in a cold room or in the fridge until the whey drains – for 3 hours at least.

Take out of the sieve, put on a round plate and garnish. Store in the fridge.

My sister's apple pie

Knead short-crust pastry, i.e. mix the flour and baking powder with butter, sugar and vanilla sugar. Add the yolks and knead. Cut off and set aside ⅓ of the dough and use the rest to form the bottom of an apple pie in a baking in. Mix the washed, peeled apples, grated using a large-hole grater, with the sugar and cinnamon, stew slightly over a low heat without a lid. Place the cooled apples on the short-crust pastry, cover with the remaining ⅓, put in a preheated oven and bake for about an hour at 180°C. When it cools sprinkle with icing sugar.

This a delicious apple pie, but my recipe is a little bit different. On short-crust pastry (made according to the same recipe) I put pieces of raw apples, sprinkle them slightly with lemon juice and a bit of icing sugar and cinnamon. I grate frozen dough over it (⅓) and put in the oven.

½ kg flour

200 ga of butter

¾ glass of sugar

3 yolks

1 tbsp of double cream

1 tsp of baking powder

1 tsp of vanilla sugar

fat and breadcrumbs for the mould

1 kg apples (Antonovka or Reinette apples)

½ glass of sugar

a pinch of cinnamon

icing sugar

½ kg flour

200 g of butter

1 egg

1 yolk

50 g of yeast

1 tsp of sugar

½ tsp of salt

½ glass of milk

Stuffing:

plum jam, pieces of apples or cheese

Crescent rolls

Sift the flour, add the fat and the egg and mix to give it a "sandy" consistency. Add the yeast, sugar and a pinch of salt to warm milk, stir and pour into the flour. Knead and form the dough into a ball. Put in a dish filled with cold water. When it floats to the surface take it out of the water and place on a pastry board sprinkled with flour. Divide into 2 parts, roll out into layers about 1-cm thick and divide into 8 parts. Put the stuffing on the dough and place in a preheated oven. Bake for about 20 minutes at 180°C.

My aunt's angel wings

Sift the flour and add the yolks, sugar, cream, alcohol and melted butter. Knead the dough thoroughly and pound using a rolling pin, i.e. let it breathe. Leave in the fridge for an hour, then tear off piece by piece and roll out into thin layers. Angel wings are more delicious when the dough is thinner. Cut into thin strips. The width depends to a great extent on your patience. The dough has to be thin, but angel wings must not break on the way to the mouth, so they need to be a maximum of 3-4 cm wide and 10-12 cm long. Make a slit in the middle of each rectangle and run one tip of the dough through it. Place on a pastry board. Melt the fat in a low saucepan and put in the angel wings when it's very hot. Bake until light golden and scoop out carefully, keeping over the saucepan for a while for the fat to drain off. Arrange on a serving plate in layers and sprinkling with icing sugar.

½ kg flour

4 tbsp of cream

6 yolks

2 tbsp of icing sugar

4 tbsp of vodka

50 g of butter

4 tbsp of water

700 g of cooking lard

Pickled mushrooms

1 kg wild mushrooms (chanterelles, saffron milk caps, ceps, slippery jacks)

2 glasses of water

1 glass of 10% white vinegar

a few bay leaves

a few seeds of allspice

a few peppercorns

salt, pepper

The marinade can be very sour or mild-flavoured, more spicy or sweet, made with or without slices of onion and even with the addition of aromatic pine needles.

Wash the cleaned mushrooms (cut into small pieces) and blanch in salted boiling water. Depending on the size and type, from 5 (saffron milk cap) to 20 minutes (chanterelles). Drain off and place in scalded jars. Make the marinade from two glasses of water, a glass of vinegar, salt, pepper, allspice and bay leaves. Pour the hot marinade over the mushrooms so that they are submerged in the liquid. Screw the lids on, move each jar to hear a hissing sound, screw on tightly and place upside down to cool, or pasteurize for about 10 minutes in a pot of boiling water, placing the jars on a cloth.

Mild marinades with a small amount of vinegar require pasteurizing. You can leave the jars in the pot until they cool.

Pickled cucumbers

The cucumbers should be young, green, firm and quite small, as they are easier to fit into jars and they taste better. Wash them and put into scalded and cooled down jars, adding a small sprig of garden dill, two cloves of garlic (depending on the jar size), two slices of horseradish root and a few mustard seeds (the best way is to put the spices at the bottom of each jar and cover them with the cucumbers). It always pays to experiment to find the best flavour, adding different spices to each jar, i.e. a few peppercorns, allspice, bay leaves, cherry, currant or oak leaves. Success depends mostly on the quality of the cucumbers, though. If you are not sure whether the cucumbers are firm enough, leave them in cold water for half an hour. Put them into scalded jars and cover with natural mineral water mixed with salt in a proportion of 4 g of salt per litre of water. Another way is to pour boiled, cooled down water with salt over them. Screw the lids on the jars and leave for two days at room temperature, then screw tighter and if possible keep at a lower temperature.

cucumbers

dill

garlic

mustard seed

a piece of horseradish root

40 g of salt per litre of water

Fresh pickled cucumbers

1 kg cucumbers

a few cloves of garlic

2 sprigs of dill with flowers

a leaf or a piece of horseradish root

2 tbsp of salt

Wash the cucumbers and place in a glass or stoneware dish, interleaving them with the washed dill, cloves of garlic and horseradish. Cover with mineral water mixed with salt in a proportion of 2 tbsp of salt per litre of water. Cover with a plate and load down with a scalded stone. They are edible a mere couple of hours later. They taste best two days after pickling. You can also add cherry leaves and mustard seeds.

Traditional horseradish

Soak the horseradish root in cold water, wash and peel. Boil half a glass of water with white wine vinegar, a tsp of salt and a tsp of sugar. Immediately put the grated horseradish (using a thick grater) into the hot, but not boiling marinade, so that it doesn't change colour. Mix, put into scalded jars, screw scalded lids on and leave upside down to cool.

½ kg horseradish

½ glass of white wine vinegar

1 tsp of salt

1 tsp of sugar

Cherry preserve

Wash, drain off and pit the cherries and cover them with sugar. Leave for 3-4 hours to release the juice. Scald a lemon, peel thinly (without the white pulp) and cut into thin strips. Candy the cherries with lemon zest for a few minutes over a low heat, moving the pot from time to time, and then set aside for a couple of hours. Repeat the steps, adding crushed cloves and candied fruit until the fruit becomes glassy. Pour into scalded jars, screw scalded lids on and put upside down to cool.

There are many recipes for cherry preserves. The most popular are:
- pour sugar over cherries and wait until they release the juice, then candy a few times, cooling each time;
- put into a hot syrup, leave for 3-4 hours and candy a few times;
- put into a cold syrup, leave for 3-4 hours, candy a few times, adding a little citric acid at the end.

You can also pour half a glass of brandy over the cherries before you make the preserve.

1 kg of cherries

600 g sugar

1 lemon

3 cloves

a level tsp of:

    cloves

    cinnamon

    marjoram

    peppermint

    thyme

    rhubarb root

    wormwood

1 glass of sugar

½ litre of water

1 litre of vodka

    a tsp of saffron and lavender flower

$\mathscr{B}$enedictine®

Put the spices (without the saffron and lavender) into a jar, pour in hot syrup and, once cooled, add the alcohol, stir well and set aside (for an hour) so that the ingredients fall to the bottom. Add the saffron and lavender, stir, filter, pour into bottles and store for a couple of months.

As Benedictine is one of the most popular fruit liqueurs there are many recipes for it. In one of them you add a tsp of saffron, angelica root, juniper berriesseeds, half a vanilla pod, steep it with rum and set the liqueur aside for three days, then add syrup (from half a litre of water and half a glass of sugar) and a litre of alcohol.

$\mathscr{C}$ornelian cherry liqueur

This is one of the most delicious liqueurs, but the Cornelian cherries must be ripe and can be picked only when it falls from the shrub.

1 kg Cornelian cherries

1 litre of vodka

½ litre of spirit

½ kg sugar

Pour the Cornelian cherries (rinsed, dried and pricked or slightly crushed) into a jar, steep in vodka and spirit, close tightly and leave in a warm place. After one month add sugar and set aside again for two weeks. Filter and pour into bottles, and store in a cool, dark place. The liqueur will be tastier if you add five tbsp of dried blueberries or thin lemon peel to the fruit. The longer it waits, the more aromatic it becomes. The fruit can be steeped in alcohol again, so that after a month you will get an excellent, if a bit less aromatic and less intensely coloured drink.

A mixture of Cornelian cherries and ordinary cherries also produces liqueurs in great flavours.

1 kg quince
½ litre of vodka
1 litre of spirit
1 glass of sugar
1 glass of water

Quince liqueur

This is one of the most delicious liqueurs, and is due to the fruit used. If it ripens in the sun, it gives off a splendid aroma. You can't use ripe imported quince to make this liqueur.

Cut the washed and dried fruit into quarters, remove the cores, cut the fruit into small pieces, steep in alcohol and set aside in a warm place for one month. Fans of dry liqueurs should pour out a bit of the liqueur and set it aside, preferably for six months in a dark room. Add the syrup to the rest of it and set aside for two weeks, remembering to move the jar from time to time. This filtered liqueur gets better with each passing day.

The rest of the fruit can be steeped in alcohol again with the addition of lemon peel, half a vanilla pod, a few cloves and a handful of raisins. Quince is so aromatic that you can steep it with alcohol several times.

Another version is to add a glass of cognac or rum to the liqueur.

Blackcurrant liqueur

Cover the washed, dried and stemmed fruit with sugar in a jar and leave for a couple of hours, stirring from time to time so that the sugar dissolves. Put some blackcurrant leaves in, pour in the alcohol and set aside for a month in a warm place (take out the leaves after two days). Filter, pour into bottles, and store for another month in a cool room.

To make a really superb liqueur, steep the fruit with a specially prepared "listówka" (one kg of fruit, a litre of listówka, and a litre of vodka) or a sweet grass liqueur (steep a few leaves of sweet grass, a dozen or so dark juniper berries, and two tbsp of sugar in a litre of vodka and set aside for a month). You can also steep the fruit in Bison Grass vodka (Żubrówka®).

Another recipe for the liqueur is to boil a litre of fruit juice with cloves and a glass of sugar and mix it with a litre and a half of whisky when it cools.

1 kg blackcurrant
½ kg of sugar
a few blackcurrant leaves
1 litre of vodka
1 litre of spirit

Index

Author: Elżbieta Adamska
Editor: Best Text

Copyright © 2013 Firma Księgarska Olesiejuk Ltd

ISBN 978-83-274-1084-9

Layout: Studio Firet

Picture Credits: Elżbieta Adamska, Shutterstock

Printed in Poland